THE
RELEASING
OF
THE POWER

GARY E. BARNHART

DOVE MINISTRIES
800 OFFENHAUSER DRIVE, 17D
RENO, NEVADA 89511
1996

Library of Congress Catalog Card Number: 96-95455

ISBN 1-57502-410-1

All Scripture references are taken from
the New King James Version of the Bible
unless otherwise stated. Used by permission.

Printed in the United States of America
by
Morris Publishing
3212 E. Hwy 30
Kearney, NE 68847
1-800-650-7888

Dedication

*This book is dedicated with love
to my mother,
Evelyn Barnhart,
who, on the day I was born prayed,
"Lord, make him a preacher."
Her prayers and love,
along with that of my father,
Jess Barnhart,
set before me a prime example
of faithful Christian living.*

Contents

Preface

I have participated in the Pentecostal Charismatic Movement for more than 45 years. I have observed many changes. Some have been good. Others, unfortunately, have not been so good.

What disturbs me most in our day is the lack of desire for the things of the Spirit. Where is the deep hunger for God that we once knew? Where is the hunger for the infilling of His Holy Spirit? Where is the deep desire for the manifestation of the gifts of the Spirit?

Out of my deep concern about these things, in 1993 I preached a series of sermons in my church. This book evolved from that series. I have written with every believer in mind. May it encourage a holy lifestyle that will truly release the power of God in our midst. May it ignite a flaming fire of desire in our hearts for the presence of the Holy Spirit. May it empower each reader with a greater knowledge of God, of His character and of His ways. May it draw us to Him in a greater way than ever before. May it be an agent in the Hand of God to bring Holy Ghost revival to our land in these Last Days.

Acknowledgments

I want to thank everyone who participated in helping me produce this book. While preparing the sermon series, I was convinced that the material must be available in book form. But as a busy pastor, I could not neglect my people to spend the long hours a book demands. It's a big leap from a Sunday sermon to a book! But God made a way! He nudged various people to help. A group of dedicated *Holy Ghost Writers* transcribed my sermon tapes. They include Margaret Bridge, Betty Cobb, Barb Hiscott, Jean Laderoute, Suellen McManus, Joann Prather, and Chris Stubbs. Then Susan Hyatt gave editorial assistance and formatted the material for publication.

I especially want to give a lot of love and appreciation to my wife Helen who stood with me over these many months of writing and fund raising.

Thank you.

Introduction

Christianity without the Pentecostal experience is something I cannot imagine. Mother and Dad came into Pentecost when I was about four years old. It's all I've ever known.

Pentecost stands for the matchless power and the abundant fruitfulness of the Holy Spirit outpoured in our lives. Today, perhaps as never before, we need that power and fruitfulness in our churches and in our personal lives.

The Pentecostal experience is God filling us to overflowing with His Holy Spirit. This infilling or *baptism* provides an intimacy with the Lord that is not available any other way. Through this *baptism*, we receive various supernatural gifts of knowledge and power. God gives these gifts only to those who are saved by the Blood of the Lord Jesus Christ.

He gives the gifts for one main purpose. That purpose is to empower believers with his own mighty power. This power enables the Body of Christ to carry out the will of God on earth.

Regrettably, the church today tends to quench the Holy Spirit's power! In some cases, when the Spirit begins to move, an usher might approach the "unruly" person who is so obviously moved by the manifest presence of the Lord. "Brother, be quiet!" "Sister, calm down! You're disturbing the service!"

Meanwhile, as the church suppresses the manifestations of the Spirit, the world is inviting the manifestations of Satan's power. Now, Satan has ominous power, but he can operate that power only to the extent that he is permitted to do so. The Church, you see, has God-given authority to prevent Satan's activity. If only believers would exercise that authority!

Why don't we have more Holy Ghost power in our midst? For one thing, disobedience short circuits His power. Unholy lifestyles hinder His flow in our lives. Sometimes we're just plain ignorance! Other times it's that we don't want the responsibility that accompanies the privilege of operating in the power of God.

Folks! It's time to get rid of every hindrance! Let's repent and let the power of God flow. Let's return, with all our hearts, to the Lord. Let's turn from self and be taught of Him. Let's live in such vital union with Him that we are truly vessels of honor endued with His mighty and matchless power.

Chapter 1

Fire and Wind

God's Spirit has the power to revolutionize our lives. He alone can save us and make us brand new creatures in Christ. Only He can remove the pains of life and give us His peace that passes all understanding. Only He can lift the heavy burdens and fill us with His indescribable joy.

This Holy Spirit revolution happens when we live in His presence and cooperate with Him. When we praise the Lord, His Spirit comes. When we listen to anointed preaching, the Spirit works through the Word telling us things we didn't know before and explaining how to do things we didn't know how to do. He energizes us, encourages us, and lifts us from defeat to victory. In His presence, the burdens of life take wing. From Him, we receive new strength and hope in the face of impossibilities, and we gain new insights and strategy for victorious living. By the power of the Holy Spirit, we are changed and we then become instruments of change in a troubled and hurting world.

Yes, it's so good to praise the Lord! When we can be in an atmosphere where the Holy Spirit is in control, He revolutionizes our lives.

The Pentecostal Book

The Book of Acts tells of the outpouring of the Holy Spirit on the Day of Pentecost and on the first believers. As Spirit-baptized believers today, we Pentecostals have a special love for the Book of Acts. We might call it *The Pentecostal Book.*

Every Pentecostal knows Acts 1:4 by heart!

Acts 1:4 And being assembled together with them He commanded them not to depart from Jerusalem but to wait for the promise of the Father which he said you have heard from me, for John truly baptized with water but you shall be baptized with the Holy Spirit not many days from now.

In this verse, the Resurrected Lord was about to ascend to Heaven, so what He was telling His disciples was very important. They had already been saved and baptized in water, and He was explaining to them that they would have another crucial experience. They would be baptized in the Holy Ghost and this baptism would result in new power in their lives.

Jesus gave them both a promise and a command. The promise was, *You shall receive power from on high when the Holy Ghost comes upon you (Acts 1:8).* The command was, *"Don't leave Jerusalem until the Holy Spirit fills you" (Acts 1:4).*

As Pentecostals, we believe that this verse teaches that the baptism of the Holy Spirit is an experience apart from the new birth experience. We believe it tells us that the baptism of the Spirit *follows* the new birth.

Pentecostal Power

The greatest purpose of the Holy Spirit in our lives is to give us spiritual power. He empowers us to live the Christian life successfully and to witness effectively. If we have the fullness of Spirit, His anointing and power will be obvious on our lives.

To illustrate this point, let's liken a believer to a cup. A cup is designed to hold a liquid such as water. If the cup has water in it, the water can be poured out, but if the cup is empty, it cannot be poured out! There's nothing to pour! You can't pour water from an empty cup. Yet that is what some believers are trying to do when they claim to have the Holy Spirit but, in reality, don't!

Some folks come to church and say, "Thank God I am saved and filled with the Holy Ghost. I speak in tongues." Yes, we may speak in tongues, but there's much more to being filled with the Holy Spirit than speaking in tongues! When we are truly filled with the Holy Spirit, the power of the Spirit pours out from us as a testimony to Jesus to help other people as Jesus did when He walked the earth.

As Pentecostals who love the Lord, we need to take a long, hard look at ourselves. We need to be willing to take a look at our churches. Are we really the full cups we claim to be? Or are we empty cups in need of filling?

More than Tongues

Speaking in tongues is an important part of our Holy Spirit experience, but we can speak in tongues without the anointing of the Spirit. Yes, we should speak in tongues, but we need more than tongues. We need the anointing of the Holy Spirit. We need the power of God.

If we are going to take our nation for God, we need His Holy Ghost power. If we are going to win our cities for God, we need His anointing. If we are going to see our families saved, we need God's power

Jesus didn't say, "Tarry in Jerusalem until you speak in tongues." He didn't say, "Wait in prayer until you speak another language." No! He said, "Tarry in Jerusalem until you are endued with power from on high." There is a big difference!

Luke 24:49 Behold, I send the Promise of the Father upon you; but tarry in the city of Jerusalem until you are endued with power from on High.

In other words, He said, "Tarry until you are totally engulfed with My power."

Good Programs and Tongue Speaking!
Or Holy Ghost Power?

As Pentecostals, we must examine ourselves. Are we truly Jesus' anointed church saturated with the awesome power of the Holy Ghost? Or are we consumed with good programs? Programs are good, but if our churches are just programs and socials, there's no Holy Ghost power.

Also as Pentecostals, we speak in tongues, but

again, do we really have Holy Ghost power? Speaking in tongues is good, but it doesn't equal Holy Ghost power. Speaking in tongues is just that--speaking in tongues!

Let's not make the mistake of thinking that speaking in tongues is our goal. As we grow older in the Lord, we should also grow up, and with growth should come an increase of the anointing in our lives. First and foremost, we must have the presence and power of the Holy Ghost working in us and through us. That will include speaking in tongues as the Holy Spirit helps us.

The point is that good programs and speaking in tongues can never take the place the power of the Holy Ghost. Let's not settle for cold, dead church services. Let's be sure we have the Holy Spirit's power and anointing in our midst.

Each One Filled

A church that is alive with the Holy Spirit consists of individuals who are alive with the Spirit. In the Book of Acts, the *Promise of the Father* (Acts 1:4), that is, the infilling of the Spirit, is offered to every believer. That was something new. In the Old Testament and in the New Testament before the Day of Pentecost, the Holy

Spirit came on special people at special times to accomplish special purposes. So now every believer is to be filled with the Holy Ghost, with His life and His power!

Churches die spiritually when individual members die spiritually. We die as individuals believers when we refuse to allow the Holy Spirit to move as He wills in us and through us. We become as cold and lifeless as ice even though we profess to be Pentecostal Christians!

Some folks attend church week after week and leave the services as defeated and powerless as they arrived! They have no power over the trouble in their lives, in their homes, and in their places of work. It doesn't have to be that way! We can all come alive with the power of the Holy Ghost! We can all come to church with high expectations that the Holy Spirit is going to move, and we'll not be disappointed!

The Works of Jesus

If we are really moving in mighty Holy Ghost power, we will see the same things happen in our midst that happened in Jesus' earthly ministry. People will be saved from sin and born again. They will be healed of sickness and diseases. They will be loosed from bondage and torment. They will be delivered from demons. In fact, if these things are not happening, the Holy Spirit is not active in the church!

Head Knowledge?
Or Personal Experience?

A tragic result of the absence of the Holy Spirit's manifest presence in our midst is that God's people fall into the traps of the enemy. For example, the spirit of worldliness gets a death grip on the church, and ministers and churches fall. It's because the Holy Spirit has been shut out!

You see, the church has the knowledge of the Holy Spirit, but knowledge is not enough. It's not enough to know about the Holy Spirit. We need to experience the Holy Spirit.

Each of us who takes the Lord Jesus Christ as Savior and Lord, is first of all, a member of the Body of Christ. Then we belong to the Church of God or whatever local body or denomination we choose. We must have the living presence of the Holy Spirit in our midst because it is not our group or denomination that saves, heals, or delivers people. It is the Holy Spirit working in us and through us Who does these wonderful deeds.

Pentecostal Priorities

Acts 1:3 To whom He also presented Himself alive after His suffering by many infallible proofs, beings seen by them forty days, and speaking of the things pertaining to the Kingdom of God.

As Jesus was talking with the disciples just before His ascent to Heaven, they started to talk to Him about the future. "Now, Lord, with the Cross behind us, will the Messianic Kingdom come?" Jesus told them it was not for them to know the future concerning this matter. Instead, He talked to them about the Holy Spirit, about the power they would have, and about why they would have such power.

When we're in tune with the Holy Spirit, you see, we're not concerned about the future because we're ready for His coming. People who are not ready for the future are the ones who worry about it. Jesus says, "Come on, let's be concerned with the Holy Spirit, not the future!"

Receive!

The manifest presence of the Spirit in our lives is not an automatic thing. God does not force Himself into our lives. He works with us and waits for us to respond to Him. When we invite Him to have His way with us, He gives and we receive, or He prompts us and we cooperate.

This principle of receiving is so basic and vital. Getting saved is an example of this. God has already provided for our salvation through the life, death, and resurrection of Jesus. We respond by inviting Him to come into our lives to take control. He then gives us salvation and we receive it.

Salvation brings with it both benefits and responsibilities. Once saved, we need to go on and ask God for all that He has for us to receive. Jesus said that those who would believe and receive would be filled to overflowing! The key is to receive.

John 7:37-38 On the last day of the feast, that great day of the feast, Jesus stood and cried out, saying, "If anyone thirsts, let him come to Me and drink. He who believes in Me, as the Scripture has said, out of his heart will flow rivers of living water." But this he spoke concerning the Spirit, whom those believing in Him would receive; for the Holy Spirit was not yet given because Jesus was not yet glorified.

It's an Experience!

When the Holy Spirit fills us, we know it! No one has to tell us! It's a definite experience.

Nowhere is the **experience** of the Baptism of the Spirit more obvious than it was on the Day of Pentecost.

Acts 2:1-4 When the day of Pentecost had fully come, they were all with one accord in one place. And suddenly there came a sound from heaven, as a rushing mighty wind, and it filled the whole house where they were sitting. Then there appeared to them divided tongues, as of fire, and one sat upon each of them. And they were all filled with the Holy Spirit and began to speak with other tongues, as the Spirit gave them utterance.

This experience is available to every believer. In Acts 2:38, Peter says that God intends this promise to be accessible to every generation. It's for those *who are afar off. Afar off* refers to the gentiles. We are gentiles, so Peter is saying that the promise of God is for us today.

Acts 2:38 Then Peter said to them, "Repent, and let everyone of you be baptized in the name of Jesus for the remission of sins; and you shall receive the gift of the Holy Spirit. For the promise is to you and to your children, and to all who are afar off, as many as the Lord our God will call."

Called to Be Witnesses

In Acts 1:8, Jesus tells us our purpose. We are to be witnesses to Him. He also tells us that this becomes possible by the power of the Holy Spirit. In fact, only through the power of the Holy Spirit at work in our lives can the Great Commission (Mt. 28:18-20) be fulfilled.

Just what is *a witness? A witness* is a person who attests to something based on personal experience. The experience of the Holy Spirit in our lives and personal evangelism, then, are inseparable. We must have the power of the Holy Ghost inside when we go outside to witness!

I had an interesting witnessing experience recently. When I was redeeming our cans at a mechanical can-redemption machine, a young man came along with his cans. We struck up a conversation, and he told me his story. His dream was to make it on his own from Florida to Hawaii. "I made it as far as California," he said, "but now I'm living on the streets. I had used up all my money when I got here, and then I got messed up on drugs. Now I work a little, panhandle some, and cash in cans."

I felt to be straight with him, so I asked, "Do you want to get off those drugs?" I said, "Jesus will set you free if you will turn away from your sin and turn to Him."

In this situation, I felt I was to be straight with him. In other relationships, the Spirit might prompt a very different approach.

Excuses! Excuses!

The prompting and power to witness comes from the Holy Spirit. If true witnessing depended on anything else, common excuses for not witnessing might be acceptable.

Excuse #1: I don't have time.

The main excuse given for not witnessing is lack of time. What if God were to say to us, "I don't have time for you anymore"? It's not time we need! It's willingness to witness and sensitivity to the Spirit. The Spirit will give us wisdom and boldness whenever and wherever we are if we will just live in communion with Him.

Excuse #2: I don't have enough education.

The second most common excuse given for

not witnessing is lack of education. But what do we need to know to tell someone Jesus loves them? How much education do we need to tell a lost and dying generation that Jesus wants to save them? No, it is not education we need. It is the reality of the indwelling Holy Spirit. When the Holy Spirit is alive in us, we will open our mouths and say, "You need Jesus."

Excuse #3: *I'm afraid to witness.*

The third most common excuse given as an excuse for not witnessing is fear and insecurity. "I get out there and I just don't know what to say! I get so nervous!" If we will stir up the Holy Ghost in us, we'll be bold as a lion! *God has not given us a spirit of fear*, says 2 Tim. 1:6. If we will just spend time in prayer, the Spirit will strengthen us, and neither the flesh nor the devil will be able to intimidate us.

Excuse #4: *I don't know what to say.*

A fourth common excuse for not witnessing is not knowing what to say. Now, for some folks, that seems to be the only time they don't know what to say! But God has given us the ability to speak so that we can be messengers of His Gospel. The key is to allow the Holy Spirit to rise up within us and empower us. He will prompt us as to what to say, when to say it, and how to say it. We witness, not in our power, but His.

The Holy Spirit anoints us. He gives us authority and boldness to declare Jesus. He gives us the power to establish His church locally and around the world. In Acts 1:8, Jesus says He gives us power to witness in Jerusalem, that is, **locally**. He gives us power to witness in Judea, that is, **nationally**. He gives us power to witness in Samaria, that is, **cross culturally**. And He gives us power to witness to the ends of the earth, that is, **internationally**.

Our Awesome Responsibility

Being vessels filled with the power of the Holy Spirit is an awesome responsibility. It has eternal consequences. Consider Jesus' words in John 20.

John 20:21 So Jesus said to them again, "Peace to you. As the Father has sent Me, I also send you." And when He had said this, He breathed on them and said, "Receive the Holy Spirit. If you forgive the sins of any, they are forgiven them; if you retain the sins of any, they are retained."

In other words, Jesus has given us the power

of the Holy Spirit to preach both the way of salvation and the way of damnation. God is willing to entrust to us such responsibility! Let's stir ourselves up in the Holy Ghost, and be found ready, willing, and able to carry out His will.

Chapter 2

Jellyfish Church
or
Pentecostal Power House?

The Jellyfish Church is a powerless entity floating down the stream of life, but the truly Pentecostal Church is a house full of the power of God. A burst of Holy Ghost power makes all the difference! We'll have that burst of power when we get fed up with the world and turn to God with all our hearts. He comes when we say, "Holy Spirit, take over. Come into my life. I'll be what You want me to be, dear Lord."

Let's get back to being a church filled with the power of Pentecost. It was the Holy Spirit Who attracted the throngs of people. They asked, "What is this?" And when Peter preached to them, multitudes were saved.

Those crowds weren't attracted by a church social. And crowds will not be converted today by church socials or baseball games or movies or any other cleverly devised programs. They'll be attracted by the same thing that attracted the crowds on the Day of Pentecost. It was the power of the Holy Spirit demonstrated in the lives of everyday people that drew the crowds to see what was happening.

Keys to Holy Ghost Power

We can discover what made the early church great. In fact, our church can be as great as the early church was because the same Holy Spirit that was available to them is still available to us. Our part is to seek the Lord with the same fervor as they did. Our part is to stir up the power of the Holy Ghost in us as they did.

If we are not experiencing the things those early believers did, we can. We can pray as they did. We can have what they had. We can do what they did.

Acts 1:12-14 tells about the believers' *Upper Room Prayer Meeting* after they saw Jesus ascend to Heaven. In this passage, we can discover-several keys to their success.

Acts 1:12 They had returned from the mount which is a Sabbath day's journey and when they had entered they went up in the Upper Room where they were staying. There were Peter, James, John, Andrew, Philip, and Thomas, Bartholomew, Matthew, James, the son of Alphaeus, and Simon the Zealot, and Judas the son of James. They continued with one accord in prayer and supplication with the women and Mary the mother of Jesus and with his brothers.

Key #1: Tarry in Prayer.

Notice how those believers tarried in prayer. They weren't preoccupied with what they were going to do after the meeting. Nor were they preoccupied with what other people were doing. They were focused on the Lord!

Key #2: Pray in Unity.

Notice, too, how those first believers were in one accord in prayer. They were not squabbling. They were in harmony, seeking God for an out-pouring of the Holy Ghost! We can be in unity and harmony too! In fact, if we don't get in harmony, the time will surely come when we'll wish we had!

Key #3: Obey the Lord Jesus.

Notice how they were obedient to the command Jesus had given them. He had commanded them to go to Jerusalem and tarry (Acts 1:4), and they obeyed. We too need to be where He tells us to be and we need to be doing what He tells us to do. How we need to learn that lesson of obedience!

Key #4: Pray Fervently and Persistently.

One thing is certain! The Holy Spirit must be alive in our midst. That takes fervent, persistent prayer. Among the early believers, there was one kind of prayer and that was fervent, believing, persistent prayer. That's the only kind of prayer that will bring a move of the Holy Spirit.

God is looking for people He can bless. He's not going to send His Spirit on worldly people. He will come to holy, pure, consecrated people. He will come to praying people.

A Church with Backbone!

Prayer puts spiritual backbone in a church. That's the kind of church Jesus is coming for! He's not coming for a jelly fish church, a church with no back bone! He's not coming for a church that wobbles and waffles! He's coming for a powerful church, a church filled with His Holy Spirit.

A praying church is an overcoming church. We have an adversary, the Devil. We don't talk to him kindly. No! We rise up in the power of the Holy Ghost, and boldly command him to flee! We let him know who's in charge! That's possible only as the Holy Spirit lives in us.

God doesn't want us to whine and beg in prayer. He expects us to be bold in spirit and fervent in prayer. We don't beg Him to save our families or heal a loved one. No! We rise up in the authority of the Holy Spirit in us, and we win the lost, heal the sick, and cast out devils. We have the power to reach out our hands and say, "Be healed, in the name of Jesus Christ of Nazareth!"

Parties or Prayers?

Do we go to church to party or to pray? When we go to church we need to gather at the altar and pray for the outpouring of the Holy Spirit. When we do that, if someone in the congregation needs to get saved, the power of God will convict that person of sin and convince him or her of the saving power of the blood of Jesus Christ. An altar call won't even be necessary! People will run to the altar to get saved! People will get healed sitting in their seats! They'll stand and shout, "I'm healed! Glory to God! I just felt the power of God go through me and I know I'm healed!"

That's what an old-fashioned Pentecostal service is like! That's the kind I grew up in! We would have a church service inbetween two fervent prayer meetings. In the "inbetween," there would be a move of the Holy Ghost. People would move as the Holy Ghost moved. Some would run. Some would be slain under the power of God. Some would speak in tongues. The Holy Ghost was alive in the church!

When the Holy Spirit comes in power, He cleanses us. He convicts us of sin, and we turn from our own ways to His. When we change, our church changes, and when our church changes, society around us changes. How the world needs to see a holy church full of the mighty power of the Holy Ghost! That's what will shut down the pornography shops. They won't even think of opening such a place when the Holy Ghost comes to town.

Moaning or Miracles?

Are you content to go to church and not see souls saved? Are you satisfied not see blind eyes made to see and deaf ears made to hear? Are you satisfied when cancer is not healed and depression is not lifted? No! A thousand times, no! A church that is alive with the Spirit experiences God's saving, healing, miracle-working power. In every service, souls are saved, sick bodies are healed, and miracles of all kinds occur.

When we go to church, we should be changed. In some significant way, we should leave better than we arrived. We should leave stirred because we've been in God's manifest presence. We should be eager to go out to share the life of Jesus, and we should be eager to get back to the next service for more!

When the Holy Spirit is alive in the midst of the congregation, there'll be no moaning and groaning. Instead, there will be a sense of expectation and faith. There will be hunger for the Word and expectation for the work of the Spirit.

A Gimmick or a Gift?

The fullness of the Spirit is a gift from God that empowers us to live and witness in Holy

Ghost power. It's a gift, so it is not earned. We receive it by faith, not by gimmicks and good works. What a gift it is!

In our town, one store started selling pornography. When I challenged them, one of the clerks said, "If you boycott our store, our business will suffer, and if that happens, I won't have a job, and my kids will suffer. I'm a widow woman and I have children to feed and clothe."

I replied, "That's all the more reason you ought to tell your boss to get the pornography out of here!"

Turning to a customer, I asked, "Do you want your daughter raped?"

"Of course not!" he replied.

"If she were raped, wouldn't you do something about it?"

"Well, yes!"

"Well, then," I said, "do something about this. With this kind of stuff, the raping is done in the mind, and then it often shows up in actual physical rape!"

Well, they were glad to see me go! But, you know, in the power of the Holy Ghost, we need to take a stand against things that are wrong. We need to take possession or our land! In the power of the Holy Ghost, we need to step out of our comfort zone and begin to do things that will make life better for everyone.

Are we ready for a Holy Ghost-anointed church filled with His power? Are we ready to get out of our self-centeredness and let the Holy Spirit have control? Are we willing to be more than pew warmers? Are we really willing to get involved with the things that move the heart of God?

God hates sin because it destroys people, and His crowning creation. The Devil is out to steal, kill, and destroy, but if we will rise up in the power of the Spirit, we have the power to defeat the devil. You know, the devil is not afraid of powerless Christians, but he is afraid of Christians who live in the power of the Spirit.

To Be Like Jesus

"Did Jesus speak in tongues?" some folks ask. The Bible doesn't tell us! We do know that He was filled with all the fullness of the Godhead; in other words, we know that He was filled with all the fullness of the Holy Spirit.

The thing to remember is that Jesus, when He was on earth, operated in the power of the Holy Spirit. Luke tells us that the Holy Spirit came upon Jesus at His water baptism. He describes the Holy Spirit, in this case, as being like a dove, a symbol of gentleness and innocence.

> *Luke 3:21 But all the people were baptized, and it came to pass, Jesus was also baptized and while He prayed, the heavens opened and the Holy Spirit descended in bodily form like a dove upon Him and a voice came from heaven which said, "You are my beloved Son in whom I am well-pleased."*

Something we should notice here is that if Jesus had to be filled with the Holy Spirit, how much more do we need that infilling! If Jesus, who was God in human form, needed the Holy Spirit, how much more do we who are born in sin need the Spirit alive in us!

It was through the Holy Spirit that Jesus did His mighty works.

> *Acts 10:38 How God anointed Jesus of Nazareth with the Holy Spirit and with power who went about doing good and healing all who were oppressed by the devil for God was with Him.*

Overcome or Overcomer?

A believer filled with the Holy Spirit cannot be possessed by the Devil. That person, paid for by the Blood of Jesus, is *possessed* by the Spirit of

God. How can bitter and sweet water proceed from the same fountain?

We do have spiritual battles, however. We are engaged in spiritual warfare, for we have an adversary, the Devil. Demonic possession can occur before we get saved or even after we get saved if we turn away from Christ. The good news is that as believers we don't need to be oppressed, depressed, or possessed.

Luke tells us how Jesus dealt with the onslaughts and schemes of Satan.

Luke 4:1   Then Jesus, being filled with the Holy Ghost returned from Jordan and was led by the Spirit into the wilderness.

In this passage, Luke tells us that Jesus went into the wilderness for forty days to fast and to pray. During that time, the Devil launched an all-out attack on Him.

First, he said, *Jesus, if you are the Son of God, command this stone to become bread (Lk. 4:3).* But Jesus had a word for him! He said, *It is written, "Man shall not live by bread alone, but by every word of God" (Lk. 4:4).*

Then he offered Jesus worldly authority.

Lk. 4:6 The devil said to Him, "All this authority I will give You, and their glory; for this has been delivered to me, and I give it to whomever I wish."

The Devil is so stupid! He offered Jesus authority! But Jesus already had **all** authority! In fact, He had already cast Satan out of Heaven! Nevertheless, Satan said to Jesus, "I'll give you authority. It has been delivered into my hand, and I give it to whomever I wish."

Jesus replied, *Get behind me, Satan! For it is written, "You shall worship the Lord your God and Him only you shall serve" (Lk. 4:8).*

Then the devil set Jesus on the pinnacle of the temple and said, *If you are the Son of God, throw yourself down from here* (Lk. 4:9).

Jesus was not stupid! He replied, *It has been said, "You shall not tempt the Lord your God" (Lk. 4:12).*

Jesus spoke with authority that far exceeded any the Devil claimed to have! The Devil only has as much power as we are willing to surrender to him. Jesus wasn't willing to give him an inch! And we shouldn't either!

Luke 4:14   Jesus returned in the power of the Spirit to Galilee, and the news of Him went out through all the surrounding region.

The work of the Holy Spirit in Jesus' life and ministry is emphasized in the Gospel of Luke.

He is the Gospel writer who makes it clear that it was after His baptism and temptation that Jesus operated in the power of the Holy Spirit. Even though Jesus was the Son of God, that alone did not make Him famous. Even the prophetic gift didn't do it! It was, instead, the mighty demonstrations of the Holy Spirit that caught the attention of the masses.

With the Holy Spirit's power in us, we too can resist Satan as Jesus did. You see, it isn't natural power that overcomes Satan because he is a spirit being. Our battle, therefore, must be waged and won in the spirit realm. That is why we need the infilling of the Omnipotent One, the Holy Ghost.

We all have our battles, but Jesus has given us power over all the power of the enemy, and if we will stand up and use it, nothing can hurt us.

The Need-Meeter

Jesus was about thirty years old when He received the empowering of the Holy Spirit and began His public ministry. Crowds gathered wherever He went because of the presence of the Holy Spirit in His life. Through that power, He met the needs of people.

Today, people still have needs. They are still

looking for answers and help. That help comes through the Holy Spirit. There is no other way. God wants to fill us with that power to save, to heal, and to help. We are His hands, His feet, His heart, His mouthpiece to a needy world.

The Jellyfish Church does not have the answer. People will not go to dead meetings that have no power to meet their many needs. Most people are busy, and they don't have time to go to meaningless services. They are tired, and they aren't interested in trying to stay awake while some people perform.

The Pentecostal Power House is a church that is vibrant with the life of the Holy Spirit. It will attract busy people who will go away revived, refreshed, and renewed.

Chapter 3

Birth of Power

Unity and Power

The Day of Pentecost marks the birthday of the Church. It brought a tremendous burst of Holy Ghost power. According to Peter, this event was foretold by the prophet Joel hundreds of years before.

Joel 2:28 It came to pass afterward that I will pour out my Spirit on all flesh. Your sons and your daughters will prophesy. Your old men shall dream dreams. Your young men shall see visions. And also on my manservants and on my maidservants I will pour out my Spirit in those days.

In looking at the record of the event in Acts 2:1-4, we are immediately struck by the fact that the disciples were in unity.

Acts 2:1-4 When the Day of Pentecost had fully come, they were all with one accord, in one place. And suddenly there came a sound from heaven, as of a rushing mighty wind, and it filled the whole house where they were sitting. Then there appeared to them divided tongues, as of fire, and one sat upon each of them. And they were all filled with the holy Spirit and began to speak in tongues, as the Spirit gave them utterances.

Unity Produces Power.

Normally, we think *with one accord* means going to church together and singing and worshipping the Lord. That may be a good start! However, the phrase actually comes from the Greek word *homothumadon* which means *being unanimous, or having mutual consent, being in agreement, having group unity, having one mind and one purpose.*

Can we honestly say this kind of unity exists in our churches today? The fact is that if we want the outpouring of the Spirit the way the early church had it, we need the kind of unity they had. We need to be in one place, unanimously together with one goal and with a determination to do what God has called us to do.

Unity Leads to Action.

It is obvious that this unity was not an end in itself. It was a unity that led to action. It led to the preaching of the Gospel and to multitudes being saved.

When we experience this kind of unity, we experience the same motivation as they did on the Day of Pentecost. We are no longer satisfied to sit around just waiting for Jesus to return. We are stirred to action. We experience hatred for sin. We experience God's love for people, and through His eye, as it were, we see their tremendous needs. We are stirred by the Spirit to see the lost saved, the sick healed, and the captives set free.

We call ourselves *Pentecostal.* It's time for *Pentecostal* unity and *Pentecostal* power in *Pentecostal* churches. The power of Pentecost is not a display of emotion, but it is a demonstration of power that changes our attitudes and actions. To experience this power, we must be willing to have Pentecostal unity. We must be willing to work together one hundred percent. What a challenge!

Tongues or Power?

We are sometimes guilty as Pentecostals of thinking that the Holy Spirit is the same as speaking in tongues. Our goal seems to be to speak in tongues, and once we do, we seem to think we've got it all. We speak in tongues, yet we are powerless because we stop seeking the Lord. Speaking in tongues should not be our goal! It is only the starting point of a living relationship with the Holy Spirit.

In this dynamic relationship, we come to know God intimately. What is the Holy Spirit really like? Who is this Holy Spirit? Who is this Person of God in us who acts and moves in such a beautiful and powerful way? Who is this One who is never rude or disruptive, and who never brings confusion?

Power in Prayer

Romans 8:27 Now He who searches the hearts knows what the mind of the Spirit is, because He makes intercession for the saints according to the will of God.

The Spirit of God knows the mind of God. Do we realize this, or do we treat the Holy

Spirit as if He doesn't know much of anything? The Spirit is all-knowing, and He lives in us!

Because the Holy Spirit lives in us, we are able to pray according to His will. The Holy Spirit makes intercession for us according to the will of God. He knows our needs better than we do ourselves! He prays for us when we can't pray for ourselves.

> *Rom. 8:26 Likewise the Spirit also helps our infirmities. For we do not know what we should pray for as we ought, but the Spirit Himself makes intercession for us with groanings which cannot be uttered.*

In this passage, the expression *which cannot be uttered* does not mean *silent*. It means *not able to be put into words*. So we need our prayer language. We need to allow the Holy Spirit to pray through us to the Father.

Sometimes we just don't know how to pray, but when we really want to pray, God enables us to pray about things on His heart. The Holy Spirit prays through us, and those things we can't put into words, He puts into expressions as we yield to Him. Sometimes we can only moan and groan! Don't be afraid of that! Just pray as He moves you to pray and the results will be wonderful!

Godly Desires

Hebrews 10:15 And the Holy Spirit also witnesses to us; for after He had said before, "This is the covenant that I will make with them after those days, says the Lord: I will put My laws into their hearts, and in their minds I will write them."

God gives us the desire to do His will. The key word is *desire*. Do we have a real *desire* to serve God? You know, many of God's people have lost that desire. It shows in their testimonies that go something like this: "Thank God for saving my soul, sanctifying me, and filling me with the Holy Ghost."

If we are alive to God, the Holy Spirit is constantly filling us with fresh and vibrant desires to do things for Him. If we are not experiencing this, we need to check up on ourselves. Do we have a desire to see souls saved? Do we have a desire to stand up and fight the fight of faith against the enemy? Do we have a desire to show the compassion of Jesus to hurting and needy people? Do we have a sense of excitement to get up and go to church? Do we have a desire to pay our tithes and to give offerings? Without such desires, what would become of the church?

How we need the Holy Spirit to fill us with fervent, fresh desire. There is so much more to Christianity than going to church meetings. That can become so empty! So powerless! Without the Holy Spirit it's all just dead religion.

The Holy Spirit is pleading for the church to awaken! He is wanting us to become warriors in the power of the Spirit in these Last Days. The choice to is ours. The Spirit is waiting for us to yield to Him and to be filled with His desires. Let's do it! Let's shake the gates of Hell!

Hearing Ears

Rev. 2:7 He who has an ear, let him hear what the Spirit says to the churches. To him who overcomes I will give to eat from the tree of life, which is in the midst of the Paradise of God.

Do we have ears to hear? God is the Great Communicator and He gives us ability to hear Him. We are His sheep who know His voice, and a stranger we'll not follow (Jn. 10:27). If we are not able to hear Him, we have probably allowed our spiritual ears to get clogged, and we need to clean them out!

This passage also tells us that God calls us to overcome. *Overcome* is a military term suggesting combat against the forces of evil. In this case, the force of evil is Satan. We are overcomers when we stand strong in faith in the midst of trials and temptations. We stand strong by putting on the whole armor of God (Eph. 6:11-17). The more we stand, the stronger our faith becomes. We pray. We listen for the Lord's commands, and we obey. We stand. We keep standing. We don't run and hide. We have nothing to fear but fear itself. We are more than conquerors through Christ. So we stand. And we win!

This passage also speaks of *Paradise*. This is a Persian word for *garden*. When we overcome, we will stand in the midst of the heavenly Garden of God! When we overcome we are assured of a place in Heaven! We win in the battles of life through the power of the Holy Spirit.

Grieving the Spirit

Our relationship with the Holy Spirit is so important. It is something we develop through time spent in prayer. The more time we spend with Him, the better we know Him. The more we develop an intimacy with Him, the more we understand His ways.

The Holy Spirit wants a personal relationship with us. He has feelings. Sometimes we act as if

He doesn't. The Bible, however, warns us not to grieve Him, and grief is an emotion.

Eph. 4:30 And do not grieve the Holy Spirit of God, by whom you were sealed for the day of redemption.

What does it mean to grieve the Holy Spirit? Simply stated, it means to cause Him injury or distress. This grief is the result of sin and disobedience. When we disobey God, we cause injury to the person of God living in us.

We grieve Him when we allow sin into our lives. For example, when we say something we shouldn't, we grieve Him. When we go places, we shouldn't, we grieve Him. The Holy Spirit wants a relationship with each one of us that is strong, pure, and holy.

Luke tells the story of two people who grieved the Holy Spirit so deeply that He took their lives (Acts 5:1-11). Ananias and Sapphira had sold a piece of property and had kept back part of the proceeds for themselves. They had taken a portion to the apostles, but were deceitful, implying they had given all. Peter confronted them individually, asking them why they had lied to the Holy Spirit. Immediately they dropped dead! God didn't take their lives for not paying their tithes. God took their lives for lying!

Isn't it amazing how we sometimes allow the enemy to distort our thinking? Here's an example of what I mean. Suppose a person makes $1000 one week. He knows he should pay $100 tithes, but instead he reasons and decides to give only $25. After all, He thinks nobody will known the difference. But the Holy Spirit knows! You see, that person hasn't lied to the church. That person has lied to the Holy Spirit. And that is a dangerous thing to do!

Submitting to the Spirit

We grieve the Holy Spirit when we do not submit to Him. But what does it mean to submit to the Holy Spirit? Paul shows us the relationship between being filled with the Spirit and submission.

Eph. 5:18- 21 Be filled with the Spirit, speaking to one another in psalms and hymns and spiritual songs, singing and making melody in your hearts to the Lord, giving thanks always for all things to God the Father in the name of our Lord Jesus Christ, submitting to one another in the fear of God.

The most important thing is not our submission to the church or to one another. The important thing is our submission to God. When we submit to God, it follows that we will submit to one another. When we do not totally submit to what is written in God's Word, we don't submit in other things, but once we submit to His Word, everything else will take care of itself.

Our best defense against this sort of self-deception is through mutual accountability. We grow in being accountable as we renew our mind in God's Word. Through God's Word, we realize we cannot lie to the Holy Ghost and get away with it. He knows exactly who we are and what we do.

When we submit to God it follows that we will submit to those who are over us in the Lord, and we will submit to one another. It is all the result of submitting to God. When we do not totally submit to what is written in God's Word, we don't submit in other things, but once we submit to His Word, everything else will take care of itself.

Chapter 4

Power Revealed

Power Gifts

1 Cor. 12:11 But one and the same Spirit works all these things, distributing to each one as He wills.

According to this passage, the Holy Spirit works in us and through us by giving us spiritual abilities called *gifts*. They are called *gifts* because we do not earn them. We do not choose them. God gives them to each believer as He sees fit.

1 Cor. 12:8 But to one is given the word of wisdom through the Spirit, to another the word of knowledge through the Spirit, to another faith by the same Spirit, to another gifts of healings by the same Spirit, to another the working of miracles, to another prophecy, to another discerning of spirits, to another different kinds of tongues, to another the interpretation of tongues.

Paul says that God gives us gifts as He wills, not as we will. It's **as He wills.** Sometimes we wonder why we don't have certain gifts. God, in His great wisdom, knows what we can handle best. The Spirit is poured out on all believers, but the gifts vary according to the individual.

Some folks use the gifts as **they** will, rather than as **God** wills. This can happen because when God gives gifts, He does not take them back (Rom. 11:29). Our responsibility is to use them according to His leading, but some folks use them independently because of the attention it gets them. This is wrong and dangerous!

Prophesying

2 Peter 1:21 For prophecy never came by the will of man, but holy men of God spoke out as they were moved by the Holy Spirit.

A prophecy is a specific message that tells us precisely what God wants to say. All prophecies must agree with the Bible. The Old Testament prophets spoke as the Holy Spirit guided them. That is how prophecy comes today. The Holy Spirit stirs in us and prompts us to speak a word of uplift. Prophecy that is truly inspired by the Holy Spirit will not tear down or destroy. It will not render harm or embarrassment. It is, instead, a vehicle of encouragement, strength, and revelation.

A Power-full Relationship

Our Teacher

John 14:26 But the helper, the Holy Spirit, whom the Father will send in my name, He will teach you all things and bring to your remembrance all things that I said to you.

According to this passage, the Holy Spirit is our Teacher. Some people think this means we do not have to study, but that is not the case. He tells us how we ought to live. He directs our thinking as we read the Bible. In daily life, He brings to your remembrance all the things Jesus has said to us. He's telling us that He will bring the Word of God to our remembrance. That is why it is so important to know the Bible.

The Holy Spirit brings to our remembrance Scriptures appropriate to our particular situation. For example, when we are attacked by the enemy, He reminds us that we have authority. He bids us arise and say, *It is written. . . . Satan, get behind me!* In the same way, when a person comes against us, the Holy Spirit will help us.

He reminds us of Scriptures that provide comfort and protection, or that impart wisdom and direction.

Our Helper

The Holy Spirit is Our Helper. He's in us, with us, and for us, helping us in all the affairs of life. How many times we would have lost the battle without Our Helper! We just wouldn't make it without the Holy Spirit! He's standing with us. He's standing in us. He's standing before us helping us to be what we need to be. He is Our Helper.

Our Advocate

The Holy Spirit is Our Advocate? *An advocate* is one who pleads our case. He is one who speaks on our behalf and intercedes for us.

Our Guide

The Holy Spirit will nudge us, speak to us, and in every possible way, guide us in the way we should go. He will not forsake us in any way (Heb. 13:5-6). Yet, so often, we get off track and miss God's best. If we would only pay attention to the Holy Spirit, that would not happen!

It sounds so easy! But, you know, we all miss it from time to time. How many times have we thought we knew the leading of the Lord, but we were dead wrong? It takes a lot of praying, a lot of time listening to God and talking to Him, to know Him intimately.

Sometimes we mistake the Holy Spirit for emotion, or emotion for the Holy Spirit. He influences our emotions, but He is far more than emotion. The Holy Spirit is our source of truth and spiritual understanding. The Holy Spirit lifts up Jesus and sets us free from all bondage to self, other people, and demons. He builds us up and enables us to live the Christian life.

Sometimes the Holy Spirit alerts us to do something, and sometimes He commands us not to do a thing. An example of this is in Acts.

Acts 16:6-7 Now when they had gone through Phrygia and the region of Galatia, they were forbidden by the Holy Spirit to preach the word in Asia. After they had come to Mysia, they tried to go into Bithynia, but the Spirit did not permit them.

How many times have we felt the Holy Spirit telling us to do something and we just didn't do it? Why does he do it? He keeps doing it because He cares about us. He patiently directs us for our own good.

It seems to be part of being human to tell others what to do. We just like to do that, don't we? But the Holy Spirit is different. He only does it when He must! When He commands us it is for our good!

A Serious Charge!

Matt. 12: 31 Therefore I say to you, every sin and blasphemy will be forgiven men, but the blasphemy against the Spirit will not be forgiven men.

Blasphemy is a very serious charge! But these people were not ignorant. They knew what they were doing! How many of us also plead ignorance in times of disobedience? How many of us say, "I didn't know what I was doing!"? And we try to excuse our lazy, irresponsible ways.

Perhaps this is somehow related to our culture or to the laws in our nation today. It seems criminals can get away with anything, even murder! Yes, they committed some terrible act, but they plead they should not be held accountable because they themselves are victims of society. Or they plead innocence on the basis of insanity. Their mind snapped under stress, they say. They weren't thinking clearly when they committed a heinous crime. It is always somebody else's fault. What ever happened to a sense of personal responsibility?

In their charge of blasphemy against Jesus, the Pharisees knew what they were doing.

Matt. 12:24 But when the Pharisees heard it they said, "This fellow does not cast out demons except by Beelzebub, the ruler of the demons.

In this passage, they were intentionally attributing the work of the Lord to the Devil. They knew what they were saying. Their sin was not a result of society or insanity. It was, instead, the continual and willful rejection of the truth. It was sin. They knew the truth, but they chose to insult the Holy Spirit. This is the sin that will not be forgiven.

These Pharisees knew what was right and wrong, but they made a decision to say that good was evil and evil was good. They called the Spirit of God the spirit of Satan. Let's learn from their mistake and not be guilty of such awful treatment of God. We only hurt ourselves! In fact, no one ever benefits.

When we reject the Spirit, we are rejecting God. The Spirit possesses the divine attributes of the Godhead. Let's not grieve Him!

The All-Powerful One

He Is Always Present.

The Holy Spirit is eternal. He was there in the beginning when God created all things and said, *Let us make man in Our image* (Gen. 1:27). He will be there at the Great White Throne when all people will stand before Jesus to be judged.

The Bible tells us we cannot get away from the Holy Spirit. In Psalm 139:7, David says *Where can I go from Your Spirit? Or where can I flee from Your presence?* In other words, the Spirit of God is always and everywhere present. We cannot escape His Presence. He is *omnipresent* which means He is everywhere present. We cannot hide from the Holy Spirit. He sees everything all the time.

He Has All Power.

Luke 1:34-35 Then Mary said to the angel, "How can this be, since I do not know a man? And the angel answered and said to her, "The Holy Spirit will come upon you, and the power of the Highest will overshadow you; therefore, also, that Holy One who is to be born will be called the Son of God."

This passage shows us that the Holy Spirit is *omnipotent* or all powerful. He has the power to cleanse us from all sin. He has the power to heal us from all sickness. He has the power to deliver us from all evil. The Holy Spirit has the power to pull down the strongholds that are binding the churches, and that are binding families. The Holy Spirit is all powerful!

He Knows Everything.

1 Cor. 2:10 But God has revealed them to us through His Spirit.   For the Spirit searches all things, yes, the deep things of God.

The Holy Spirit is *omniscient*, or all-knowing. He knows every thought we think. Sometimes the Devil tempts us to think his thoughts, but we always have a choice. We can reject those thoughts that come to distract us from godly thoughts. The Holy Spirit knows all about what is going on in our minds. We cannot hide our thoughts from the Holy Spirit.

Power Symbols

Wind

Acts 2:1-2 Now when the Day of Pentecost had fully come, they were all with one accord in one place. And suddenly there came a sound from heaven, as a rushing mighty wind, and it filled the whole house where they were sitting.

The power of the Holy Spirit is pictured as wind. It's not ordinary wind, however! The Spirit comes as extraordinary wind, as a rushing, mighty wind. He is the unseen power of God.

Fire

The power of the Holy Spirit is also pictured as fire. When Moses was tending the flock of Jethro, his father-in-law, on the backside of the desert, the Lord appeared to him as a flame of fire (Ex. 3:1-3). But the bush wasn't burning! The bush was not consumed. What was this? It was the glory of God's presence, the Shekinah glory of God. The fire is the symbol of Divine Presence.

There is nothing like the fire of the Holy Ghost. He did not leave us without fire. Nor did He leave us with just a little feeling. He gave us the fire!

Water

Jn. 7:37-38 On the last day, that great day of the feast, Jesus stood and cried out, saying, "If anyone thirsts, let him come to Me and drink. He who believes in Me, as the Scripture has said, out of his heart will flow rivers of living water."

Have you ever noticed the power of water? In this passage, the power of the Holy Spirit is likened to water. Have you ever watched water flowing from a dam? It flows with such force, yet the dam controls the flow. That's how it is with the Holy Spirit in our lives. We determine how much can flow out from us. We control the flow of the Spirit in our lives.

It's the same in the church The church controls the flow of the mighty force of the Holy Spirit. We control how much the Holy Spirit is able to do in our midst by how much we let Him flow through us.

But the Holy Spirit does not force Himself on anyone. We either accept Him or we don't accept him. He doesn't force Himself on us. It's our decision to let Him flow. It's up to us to cooperate with Him.

Seal

Eph. 1:13-14 In Him you also trusted, after you heard the word of truth, the gospel of your salvation; in whom also, having believed, you were sealed with the Holy Spirit of promise, who is the guarantee of our inheritance until the redemption of the purchased possession, to the praise of His glory.

Eph. 4:30 And do not grieve the Holy Spirit of God, by whom you were sealed for the day of redemption.

Power is released through authority, and *sealing* symbolizes authority. To be sealed by the Holy Spirit is to be an authorized representative of Jesus Christ. You are an official representative of heaven on earth! You are somebody! That's why we should not say, "Oh I'm nobody." No! The Bible says we are authorized representatives of Christ by the power of the Holy Spirit.

Sealing brings authority. Acts 19:1-6 tells how the Ephesians, who had already believed on Jesus, received the fullness of the Holy Spirit after Paul taught and ministered to them. In other words, they were sealed.

Healing Oil

Acts 10:38 How God anointed Jesus of Naz-

areth with the Holy Spirit and with power, who went about doing good and healing all who were oppressed by the devil, for God was with Him.

The power of the Holy Spirit to heal is symbolized as Healing Oil. The Oil continues to flow. The Spirit continues to bring healing, miracles, and deliverance to those who believe. Even now, as you read, you can receive deliverance through the Healing Oil of God. Just reach out and take it, in Jesus' name.

A Dove

John 1:32 And John bore witness, saying, I saw the Spirit descending from heaven like a dove, and He remained upon Him.

When John saw the Spirit descend from heaven like a dove and abide on Jesus, he knew with a certainty that Jesus was the Son of God. A dove symbolizes the gentleness and sensitivity of the Spirit. It portrays the power under discipline or meekness.

Yes, Holy Spirit!

Friend, today there is a need for renewal of mission and purpose in the Church. There is a need for the renewal of the dynamic power of the Holy Spirit. The power of the Holy Spirit will transform and empower the church today as it did in the early church.

The church needs the spiritual power for intensified service. We need to return to the traditional Pentecostal movement to experience a restoration of prayer, fasting, worship, the gifts of the Spirit, and holiness of life. We need to be filled with the Holy Spirit.

> *Eph. 5:18 And do not be drunk with wine, in which is dissipation; but be filled with the Spirit.*

Dissipation means *evil* or *indulgence in pleasure*. The Word tells us to be filled with the Spirit, and this does not stop with a single experience. We are to be being filled continually. We do this by singing praise and giving thanks to God, and by keeping the Word of God alive in our hearts and minds. We do it by spending time at the altar of our local church, by giving ourselves to others, and by yielding to the Spirit in prayer. This infilling of the Holy Spirit is a continual flow just as a spring of water must have a continuous flow from its source.

The Lord is looking for people who will turn to Him and be filled with His Spirit. He is looking for people who will be His power houses in the earth today. Are we willing to be those power houses individually, and are we willing, together, to be those power houses as congregations and denominations? Are we willing to say YES to the Holy Spirit?

Chapter 5

Miracles Begin

One day Peter and John were going to the temple when a crippled beggar asked them for money (Acts 3:1-10). Peter looked at him and shouted, *Look at us! Silver and gold I do not have, but what I have I give you. In the name of Jesus Christ of Nazareth, rise up and walk!* Then grasping the man's hand, he lifted him to his feet, and immediately he was healed. Leaping and praising God, this man was a powerful witness to the throngs who gathered! What a demonstration of the awesome power of the Risen Lord!

Now, we must realize that the wisdom and power released through Peter and John was not an automatic thing. They had been in the upper room diligently seeking the Lord. That is why such power was released when they spoke. That is why they experienced such amazing results!

Notice that they did more than just talk. Their actions matched their words. Peter took hold of the man's hand and, with confidence tempered by compassion, jerked him to his feet.

The same Holy Spirit is in our midst today, wanting to do the same things for us that He did for them. Those are not just nice Bible stories. They are examples of what God wants to do today. God still wants to work miracles in us and through us.

The Message Divides.

Acts 4:1-2 Now as they spoke to the people, the captain of the temple, and the Sadducees came upon them, being greatly disturbed that they taught the people and preached in Jesus the resurrection from the dead.

Then, as now, the people were sharply divided by the message. After two thousand years, not much has changed!

The religious authorities and others were so distressed that they threw Peter and John in prison (Acts 4:3-7). But nothing could stop the message, and nothing could stop the messengers, and thousands were added daily to the church.

A Prayer Life? Or a Life of Prayer?

What was the key to Peter and John's power? They were men of prayer. They didn't just have a prayer life. They had a life of prayer. As a result, they were filled with the Holy Spirit in what they said and in what they did (Acts 4:8).

Acts 4:13 Now when they saw the boldness of Peter and John, and perceived that they were uneducated and untrained men, they marveled. And they realized that they had been with Jesus.

The change in Peter and John was obvious. What had brought this change? Everyone knew that education had not been a factor in the change, for Peter and John were uneducated. They also knew sudden riches had not empowered them, for they had neither silver nor gold!

The amazing change had come because Peter and John had been with Jesus. He had given them power beyond their natural abilities. He had given them power that superseded the authority of the religious leaders. That power had, in fact, made Peter and John a threat to the religious leaders.

You know, it's not much different today. For example, we have laws and regulations against the Bible in the workplace, against preaching in the streets, and so on. Yet we can't help but speak of the things we have experienced. If you have seen Jesus, if you have felt His power, if you have felt the glorious anointing of the Holy Spirit, you have to declare it.

Again, They Prayed!

Acts 4:29-30 Now, Lord, look on their threats, and grant to Your servants that with all boldness they may speak Your word, by stretching out Your hand to heal, and that signs and wonders may be done through the name of Your holy Servant Jesus.

When Peter and John were released from jail, they told the other disciples all that had happened. They prayed for boldness. They prayed that the Lord would confirm their message with mighty signs and wonders. They wanted to see the sick healed, the brokenhearted restored, and the captives set free!

And when they had prayed, the place where they had assembled together was shaken; and they were all filled with the Holy Spirit, and they spoke the word of God with boldness (Acts 4:31).

You know, we're a bunch of weaklings! Compared with these believers, we're so timid! But may their prayer for boldness be our prayer! *Boldness is freedom of speech with frankness, cheerful courage, and absence of fear.*

What was the key to this holy boldness? It was prayer. When the persecutors tried to shut down the early church, the believers prayed. That's our key too, but many times instead of praying, we gripe and complain.

The amazing thing is that the persecution that threw Peter and John into prison was caused by one miracle, just one miracle! But that one miracle accomplished in the authority of the name of Jesus, did two things. It validated the present power of Jesus, and it fed the faith of those early believers.

The Anointed Word

The world is tired of a powerless church. It's not impressed with moaning, groaning, Sunday-go-to-meeting Christians. It's waiting to see miracles. It's waiting to see the power of God moving again as it did in the early church.

In the old days of Pentecost, if the preacher didn't shout and jump over the pews, he wasn't anointed! That might or might not be evidence of the anointing. We all have different personalities, and so we respond to God's presence in our unique ways.

If the Word of God is being preached, it's anointed because God's Word is anointed, whether I'm anointed or not! Anointing and emotion are not the same thing. There have been times that I've preached without feeling a thing, yet miracles happened all over the place! That just proved to me that it's the Word that does it, not the preacher.

Supernatural Boldness

Acts 4:31 And when they had prayed, the place where they were assembled together was shaken; and they were all filled with the Holy Spirit, and they spoke the word of God with boldness.

When they prayed, there was a supernatural shaking and they received a supernatural filling. Prayer brought a baptism of fearlessness. It's time for us to experience the same thing. It's time to get rid of our chicken costume and put on our lion's costume.

Supernatural Unity

Acts 4:32 Now the multitude of those who believed were of one heart and one soul; neither did anyone say that any of the things he possessed was his own, but they had all things in common.

These people of prayer were of one heart and mind in their attitudes and thoughts. They were in complete harmony. It was so real that they freely shared their possessions.

Supernatural Fruitfulness

Acts 4:33 And with great power the apostles gave witness to the resurrection of the Lord Jesus. And great grace was upon them all.

These people of prayer were fruitful in their witnessing. They experienced power and grace.

Supernatural Generosity

Acts 4:34-35 Nor was there anyone among them who lacked; for all who were possessors of lands or houses sold them, and brought the proceeds of the things that were sold, and laid them at the apostles' feet; and they distributed to each as anyone had need.

Look what happened in the early church because of the infilling of the Holy Ghost! Supernatural generosity flooded their lives.

Now, we say we've been filled with the Holy Spirit, but do we see that same generosity that the early church had? Do we give our tithes and offerings? Do we look after each other with that same caring and concern? In the early church, they gave to one another and made sure everyone had enough. That's one of the things that made the early church great.

Supernatural Trust in God

Do we trust God? Do we really trust Him as those early believers did? If we claim to be Holy Ghost filled believers, we should be trusting God, knowing He will do what He says in His Word.

I have always made an effort to give to God. Even when I haven't had it to give, I've given. I give because I believe that what happened in the early church happens today, and time after time I have seen God provide when there seemed to be no way. I have found that I cannot outgive God! It is so exciting. We can trust Him. He takes care of us.

Maybe all we have to give is a can of corn, a can of tomato sauce, or a package of spaghetti. Is that going to break us? No! It may not seem like much, but when everybody gives something, there's enough! God will bless you even for the fifty cent package of spaghetti! He will not let your giving go unrewarded.

Supernatural Power

Acts 4:33 And with great power the apostles gave witness to the resurrection of the Lord Jesus.

The word *power* is the Greek word *dunamis*. It also means *energy*. We have this supernatural power and energy in us! But we complain about being so tired. We're too tired to go to church or to go to the altar and pray! But the Bible says that if we're full of the Holy Ghost, we have *energy*. We have *dunamis*.

How many times have I been tired and down when the Holy Ghost has prompted me to do something. When I have obeyed, I have found new energy. *Dunamis!* Without that *dunamis*, I'm nothing, but with that *dunamis* of the Holy Ghost, I could plow down anything!

Do We Look Like the Early Church?

We need to take a good look at ourselves. Do we really look like the early church? We profess to be filled with the same Holy Ghost as those early believers were. But do we respond as they did? Do we have the power they had? Do we see souls saved by the thousands as they did? Do we experience the miracles they did?

We've made the Holy Ghost like a toy. When we want it, we pick it up and play with it. We speak in tongues, or we give a prophecy and an interpretation. Then when we don't want to play with it anymore, we lay it back down. If we're going to allow the Holy Spirit to be the main course of the Church, we must make up our minds that we're going to make a change.

Do we look at all like the believers in Acts 5?

Acts 5:12 And through the hands of the apostles many signs and wonders were done among the people. And they were all in one accord in Solomon's porch.

The power of the Holy Spirit was so great that multitudes were added to the church. They brought the sick, laid them on the street on beds and cots, and when even the shadow of Peter passed over them, they received their healing.

There was no magic in that shadow of Peter. It was the anointing of the Holy Spirit on Peter's life that brought the healings and deliverances.

Help Those Pastors!

Acts 6:1-4 Now in those days, when the number of disciples was multiplied, there arose a complaint against the Hebrews by the Hellenists, because their widows were neglected in the daily distribution. Then the twelve called the multitude of the disciples and said, "It is not desirable that we should leave the word of God and serve tables. Therefore, brethren, seek out from among you seven men of good reputation, full of the Holy Spirit and wisdom, whom we may appoint over the business; but we will give ourselves continually to prayer and to the ministry of the word."

Hellenists were Greek-speaking Jews scattered throughout the Greco-Roman world. As the church grew, many Hellenists became believers. Also as the church grew, the apostles could no longer do all that needed to be done. They quickly learned, for example, that they could not be tied down to serving tables. They could not do all that needed to be done in meeting physical needs and still prepare themselves to meet the spiritual needs of the people.

Do we want to keep our preachers weak today? Do we want to keep them overburdened and defeated? Then all we have to do is require them to do all the work of the church. If they don't have time to pray and study, they won't be ready to preach on Sunday morning, Sunday night, and Wednesday night! We shouldn't wonder why many churches never grow? They keep their pastors working a full-time job so they can live. They expect them to do all the maintenance work and all the business in addition to caring for the people.

Let's reflect on our condition. Let's repent. Let's line up our priorities with those of the early church. Let's let the miracles begin!

Chapter 6

Not for Sale!

Perhaps we don't realize how bound we are by ungodly attitudes. Ruled by the flesh and, in some cases, by the Devil, we are often infested with negative perspectives mean opinions! But when we get saved, the Holy Spirit begins to change us. He requires that we throw off our sinful, selfish ways and take on His nature. In other words, He calls us to repent.

Acts 2:38 Then Peter said to them, "Repent, and let every one of you be baptized in the name of Jesus Christ for the remission of sins; and you shall receive the gift of the Holy Spirit."

In this verse, we often place the emphasis on the word *baptism.* But the big word is *repent.* Being baptized doesn't save us, and being baptized in water doesn't cleanse us from our sins. We can be dunked a hundred times a year and still end up in hell when we die! The Bible says we must *repent.* That's the key!

In order to be filled with the Holy Spirit, we must repent. We first come to the saving knowledge of Jesus Christ. His shed blood washes away our sins. In fact, only the blood of Jesus can do this when we repent.

The *Gift* and the *Gifts*

We then receive the gift of the Holy Spirit. This is different from the *gifts* of the Spirit. *The gift of the Holy Spirit is the Spirit Himself.*

Acts 2:39 For the promise is to you and to your children, and to all who are afar off, as many as the Lord our God will call.

Peter was talking to the Jews, but he was telling them that the promise was to generations yet to come and to the gentiles. The gift of the Holy Spirit is available to all who desire it. The promise of the Holy Spirit is a gift for every believer in every generation.

This gift or *Promise of the Father* (Acts 1:4) comes to us at some point after conversion. It can also happen at the same time as conversion. I've seen people turn to Jesus, repent of their sins, and be baptized in the Holy Ghost all at the same time, and then later, they would be baptized in water. The baptism of the Holy Spirit, the infilling of the Holy Spirit, is different from salvation.

The gifts of the Spirit, on the other hand, are special abilities released in us and through us by the Holy Spirit. They've been granted to us by the Spirit to empower us for service. They are not something to be played with or mocked. They are sacred trusts to be used under the anointing of the Holy Ghost.

The Lord Jesus gives the gifts as He chooses, not as we choose. According to 1 Cor. 12, He distributes them as He sees fit.

1 Cor. 12:4-11 There are diversities of gifts but the same Spirit. There are differences of ministries, but the same glory. There are diversities of activity, but it is the same God who works all in all. But the manifestation of the Spirit is given to each one for the profit of all: for to one is given the word of wisdom through the Spirit; to another, the word of knowledge through the Spirit; to another, faith by the same Spirit; to another, the gifts of healings by the same Spirit; to another the working of miracles; to another prophecy, to another discerning of spirits, to another different kinds of tongues; to another the interpretation of tongues. But one and the same Spirit works all these things, distributing to each one indi-

vidually as He wills.

Poured out

Acts 2:33 Therefore being exalted to the right hand of God, and having received from the Father the promise of the Holy Spirit, He poured out this which you now see and hear.

Notice the expression *poured out*. The Holy Spirit doesn't come in a dribble or a little ripple! He comes like a gully-washer when we open the door and invite Him to come into our lives.

Sometimes it seems that we want a little trickle here and a little trickle there! We want just enough to make us feel good. But we need Him in His fullness! We need a pouring out of the Holy Spirit upon our souls and spirits every day.

In Pentecostal circles, we become so comfortable with the Holy Ghost. Oh, we're tongue-talkers! But we need to be more than that! We need to be filled with the Holy Ghost, and we need to live in His power all the time.

Included

Eph. 2:13 But now in Christ Jesus you who once were far off have now been brought near by the blood of Christ.

Under the New Covenant, the gentiles who believe in Jesus Christ are included in citizenship in God's kingdom. We are something altogether new under the New Covenant of Christ's shed blood. We are grafted in to enjoy all the promises of God. We are included as heirs of all His promises. What God has given to the Jews, He has given to the gentiles. He has given us His power and His promises. We're not who we used to be. We've been made new. We've been cleansed, purified, made holy. We've been anointed with the power of the Holy Ghost.

No favorites!

Acts 2:17 It shall come to pass in the last days, says God, that I will pour out my Spirit on all flesh.

In other words, this gift of the Holy Spirit is for everyone who believes. God doesn't show favoritism. He doesn't give the Holy Spirit to Africans or Americans or Russians on the basis of their race or culture. He gives the Spirit to everyone who asks.

Let's get excited about our heritage! Let's get excited about what God has given us! Let's get excited about what we can do in this world! We can change it!

I'm afraid though that too many of us like the way we live. We have grown accustomed to the mountains and the valleys. We are comfortable with roller-coaster Christianity! But let's repent and get the job done in the power of the Spirit!

Persecuted! Scattered! But not Defeated!

Acts 8:4-5 Therefore those who were scattered went everywhere preaching the word. Then Philip went down to the city of Samaria and he preached Christ to them.

Severe persecution scattered the Christians. But it did not defeat them! Is this our response to trouble and persecution?

Philip went to Samaria and preached Christ. This was the first preaching of the Good News to the gentiles. Notice that he preached Christ! He didn't preach church doctrine, legalistic habits, tradition, or politics. Philip preached Christ, and he got results!

Acts 8:6-8 And the multitudes with one accord heeded the things spoken by Philip, hearing and seeing the miracles which he did. For unclean spirits, crying out with a loud voice, came out of many who were possessed; and many who were paralyzed and lame were healed. And there was great joy in that city.

How we need this demonstration of the Spirit in our midst today! So often our efforts are fruitless, sabotaged by sin and subverted by human effort to imitate the power of God! We can change that, if we will. We can repent of our slothful ways and live in integrity. We can trust God! We can have the results Philip had. We can have that same joy in our homes and our churches as the city of Samaria experienced.

People spend great amounts of money attending seminars on successful living. As helpful as they might be, they never can get to the root of the problem and satisfy the soul. Only the presence and power of God can do that. We can receive it in the local church free for the seeking! And believe me, the money given to those seminars could be better spent in the church!

God Confirms His Word.

Mark 16:20 And they went out and preached everywhere, the Lord working with them and confirming the word through the accompanying signs. Amen.

If we want signs and wonders to follow our ministry, then we need to have a close relationship with God. Every believer is a preacher in some respect, and each of us should expect God to confirm the Good News when we share it. He doesn't confirm condemnation and fault-finding. He confirms His Word when it is preached.

What is the meaning of the word *confirm*? It means *to establish, to secure, to guarantee*. The signs and wonders established, secured, and guaranteed the message they were preaching. God was backing up their message.

Today, if signs and wonders are not accompanying our preaching, we'd better check up on what we're preaching and how we're living. The absence of signs and wonders indicates a problem! God confirmed the early church. We need His confirmation as much as they did. Let's find out where we're missing it! We want to see souls saved. We want to see the sick healed and the demon possessed delivered.

A Magician Saved

Acts 8:12 But when they believed Philip as he preached the things concerning the kingdom of God and the name of Jesus Christ, both men and women were baptized. Then Simon himself also believed; and when he was baptized he continued with Philip, and was amazed, seeing the miracles and signs which were done.

Simon had used magic for years to bewitch the Samaritans, but when he heard the message about Jesus, he believed (Acts 8:9-24). He gave up witchcraft and magic to follow Jesus.

Just as the whole town of Samaria was set free, our towns and regions can be also be set free. In the Antelope Valley of California, the region where I once lived, adult video shops began springing up, but through prayer, the power of God could have been released. It could have shut them down. The whole valley could have been changed just as Samaria was. But folks seemed to have so little concern! Wherever we live, we have the power to make the difference, but we sit in our comfortable chairs and say, "Oh well, it's really not hurting me." Yes! This sort of evil is hurting all of us! It's hurting our families, our friends, our communities.

We call ourselves Pentecostal, but do we have Pentecostal power? Should we call ourselves the *Party Gathering Church* instead! Is that more like a description of what we are doing? Is it possible we are partying on Sunday morning, Sunday evening, and during the week? It's time we got serious about God! The time is too short to continue to play!

A Gift?
Or a Reward?

Acts 8:14 -15 Now when the apostles who were at Jerusalem heard that Samaria had received the word of God, they sent Peter and John to them, who when they had come down, prayed for them that they might receive the Holy Spirit.

What exactly did they pray? They prayed that they would receive the Holy Spirit. The Samaritans had been baptized in the Name of the Lord Jesus, but the Holy Spirit had not yet fallen on any of them.

When Peter and John prayed for them, they received the Holy Spirit (Acts 8:17). It says nothing of them tarrying as they had on the Day of Pentecost. It says that Peter and John laid hands on them and prayed for them, and instantly they received.

Do you know that only fifty per cent of people who attend Pentecostal churches speak in tongues? Is it possible that we don't want the power of Pentecost?

Do you know that the size of the average

congregation in America is only 85? Would this be the case if we were experiencing Pentecostal power? Is it possible that we just want a little group where we feel safe and comfortable? Is it possible we would be upset if sinners started getting saved and coming in? How would we feel if prostitutes, homosexuals, lesbians, drug addicts, and alcoholics were to come to our church? God help us!

The way it is, it seems that we can worship God and then we can go out and live as we please. We don't want to miss our favorite TV program or our favorite ball game or our favorite party on Sunday afternoon! Our style of Christianity seems to demand nothing of us!

I'm tired of what Satan's done to our people. I'm tired of what we're allowing Satan to do in our midst. It's time to shake off those heavy weights. It's time we command Satan to pick up his weapons and flee in the Name of Jesus!

When we are baptized in the Holy Spirit after being saved, it allows what happened inside when Jesus saved us to show up on the outside. When the Holy Spirit comes alive on the inside of us, we shine as lights with the Light of the Holy Spirit. Let's not hide it!

We shine when we live openly before the Lord and people. We can't be secret Christians.

We can't party and drink on Saturday and go to church on Sunday. We can't cuss on the job. We can't walk into those X-rated places. If we're going to let our lights shine, we're going to have to live right. Let's not be hypocrites!

A Gift?
Or a Commodity?

Acts 8:18-19 And when Simon saw that through the laying on of the apostles' hands the Holy Spirit was given, he offered them money, saying, "Give me this power also, that anyone on whom I lay hands may receive the Holy Spirit."

Doesn't that sound like people today? They want to buy their way through! Some church-going folks refuse to pay tithes, while others who don't even profess to be Christians do!

I knew a bartender in St. Joseph, Missouri. Every Monday morning, he and his wife would walk to the pastor's house and pay the tithes on their hundreds of dollars of income. They believed the prosperity of their business was dependent on their paying tithes. God cannot bless that type of business even when you pay your tithes, but the devil had them fooled! How many folks have been fooled the same way?

They paid their tithes every week, but never attend church and never serve God with their lives.

When the Holy Ghost gets inside of us, we're not going to run to bars. You say, "Preacher, I don't like this old-fashioned preaching!" We may be living in the nineties, but we need to get back to this kind of preaching if we're going to have the Holy Ghost alive in our churches.

Simon wanted the power he saw demonstrated through Peter and John. But his motives were wrong! He wanted his name in lights, so to speak! He wanted people to say, "That guy who used to be a witch doctor is now causing people to receive this power."

Acts 8:20 But Peter said to him, "Your money perish with you, because you thought that the gift of God could be purchased with money! You have neither part nor portion in this matter for your heart is not right in the sight of God."

The Holy Spirit is a gift. A gift cannot be bought or earned. No amount of money can purchase the gift of the Holy Spirit. No amount of begging or bribing brings The Gift.

Chapter 7

Empowering the Church

When the Holy Ghost comes into our lives, things happen! He gives us power to live a godly lifestyle. He enables us to fulfill God's purpose in the earth. When He comes inside, it shows up on the outside.

Luke 11:9 And I say to you, ask it will be given to you; seek, and you will find; knock, and it will be opened to you. For everyone who asks receives, and he who seeks finds, and to him who knocks it will be opened.

Most of us can recite verse 9, but do we really believe what it says? Have we experienced it?

I like verse 10 because it says that everyone who asks receives. Jesus didn't say, "Ask and maybe you'll receive." He didn't say, "I hope you'll receive." He gave us clear-cut commands and wonderful promises.

Ask! Seek! Knock!

Luke 11:13 If you then, being evil, know how to give good gifts to your children, how much more will your heavenly Father give the Holy Spirit to those who ask Him!

Jesus gave the disciples these simple instructions that would result in the most powerful experience a human can have. He simply said to ask for the gift of the Holy Spirit. The key, then, to the infilling of the Holy Spirit is simply this: Ask, Seek, Knock.

Ask, seek, and *knock* (Mt. 7:7) are in the Greek present tense. In English, we think in terms of asking as a completed act, but in Greek, asking has a continuing sense. It means *to ask and to keep on asking. Seek* means *to seek and to keep on seeking. Knock* means *to knock and to keep on knocking.*

One problem we have today is that we ask once and that's it! Some recent teaching has taught us to ask God just one time for anything and then to praise Him for the answer. I believe there is some truth in that approach for some things. In this passage, however, Jesus is telling us to ask God repeatedly for what we need and desire, and then to thank Him.

Believe and Receive

People have said to me, "Pastor, I have been tarrying for the Holy Ghost for years. Why haven't I received?" Well, to be sure, desire is important, but according to these instructions from Jesus, we are to ask and to receive. Our part is to cooperate with the Spirit by receiving.

Other people say, "Pastor, if God wanted me to have the Holy Ghost, He would have given it to me." The truth of the matter is He is no respecter of persons and He wants each of us to receive the fullness of the Spirit. All we need to do is reach out and take it. It's there for us!

So many church-goers never get excited about life. How many walk around looking as if they've lost all hope! Let's get our faces turned right side up! Let's get focused on our blessings instead of being preoccupied with needs all the time! The Holy Spirit is ready to fill us and help us in every area of life!

Empowered

Acts 1:8 You shall receive power when the Holy Spirit has come upon you.

Everybody wants to be in control, and everybody wants power. Here the Scriptures tell us that legitimate power for living comes from the Holy Spirit. An important thing to remember, however, is that He has a purpose for entrusting us with His power.

The main purpose of Holy Ghost empowerment is that we might be effective witnesses to the lost. Witnessing becomes so easy and natural because we do it out of an overflow of joy and excitement. We just want to share Jesus with everyone. We want everybody to have this power and excitement that comes only from God.

No *Yo-Yos!*

When we receive this power, we have to learn to live consistently. We can't be yo-yo's for God! We can't be a Holy Ghost anointed church one day and be full of self pity the next! The Holy Ghost doesn't work that way. He's constant. He's always the same. He is the One Who lives in us and wants to live through us constantly and consistently reaching the lost.

This power that Jesus talks about in Acts 1:8 is the same power you and I hold within our tongues. We can speak God's will into existence by lining up our words with His word. Yet, how many church goers are using this incredible power to speak destruction and defeat instead of life, love, and hope. What an amazing power God has entrusted to us!

Ignited!

Mark 1:17 Then Jesus said to them, "Follow Me, and I will make you become fishers of men."

Jesus gave this command, and it remains in effect today. "Follow Me!" He says. "Together we'll win the lost." Yet the world is full of people who are dying and going to hell while we sit in our pews wanting to be entertained. We say the Holy Spirit is inside us. If that's true, we'll be concerned with the same things that concern the Holy Spirit, and the Holy Spirit is concerned about reaching lost and hurting people.

When the Holy Spirit comes inside us, we ignite! We become passionate about the things God is passionate about. He nudges us and stirs us to do His will, but He doesn't force us. He leaves it up to us. If we yield to Him, He fills us with zeal for souls.

When we look at the church, can we, in all honesty, say that we see this zeal? Or are we caught in dead formality? Are our hearts overflowing with praise, or do we just sing songs? Do we really have the guidance of the Holy Spirit, or do we lean on other people for direction? Do we get excited about going to church, or would we rather go to Disneyland? It's time to answer these difficult questions.

Purged

Matthew 3:11 [John said,]"I indeed baptize you with with water unto repentance, but He who is coming after me is mightier than I, whose sandals I am not worthy to carry. He will baptize you with the Holy Spirit and fire."

In Pentecost, when we speak of *the fire*, we think of shouting, but that's not what it really means. The fire purges and purifies us. It changes us and makes holiness a reality in our lives. It's a refining fire.

Jesus said we would be baptized in the Holy Ghost and fire. I'm not talking about emotion. I'm talking about changed lives.

How many times do people come in and get saved and filled with the Holy Spirit, but there's no apparent change in their lives. They still do the same old things they used to do! They still have the same old attitudes they used to have!

The Bible tells us the Holy Ghost and fire will change us.

Have you ever noticed how people are attracted to fire? They'll come from miles around to watch a brush fire or forest fire. I tell you, when the fire of the Holy Ghost is burning in the church, they'll do the same. People want to see what is happening when people get filled with the Holy Spirit and fire. People want to see the changed lives of God's people.

Equipped

1 Cor. 12:8-9 For to one is given the word of wisdom through the Spirit, to another the word of knowledge through the same Spirit, to another faith by the same Spirit, to another gifts of healings by the same Spirit, to another the working of miracles, to another prophecy, to another different kinds of tongues, to another the interpretation of tongues.

According to this passage, the Holy Spirit gives nine different charismatic gifts. These different expressions of the Holy Spirit must be free to operate in us if we are a going to be a charismatic Pentecostal church. In a day when many Pentecostal churches are no longer experiencing these gifts, many Charismatic church are alive with the working of the Spirit. Yet, we Pentecostals need them as much as we ever did!

These gifts can operate only through clean vessels. Some leaders in the Charismatic Movement seem to believe that the gifts will operate apart from a holy lifestyle, but sin in a person's life will hinder their expression. They are expressions of God, and God cannot live in the midst of sin. There must be a cleansing in our lives.

The Word of Wisdom

Definition: The word of wisdom is a spiritual utterance at a given moment given through the Spirit supernaturally disclosing the mind, purpose, and will of God for a specific situation.

The Word of Knowledge

Definition: The word of knowledge is a supernatural ability given by the Spirit to a specific person disclosing information about a person or event and usually having to do with an immediate need.

In one particular service when I was holding evangelistic meetings in Torrance, California, God gave me a wonderful word of knowledge for a woman who came for prayer. She said, "We have bills that have to be paid tomorrow and we don't have the money to pay them. Please pray for God to do a miracle." God said, "Tell her there will be a check in the mail tomorrow that will pay the bills." And there was! Hallelujah!

The Gift of Faith

Definition: The gift of faith is faith that God deposits in us for a particular need. It goes beyond natural faith and saving faith. It is a supernatural trust. This is the kind of faith that has no doubts. Even when circumstances say we are defeated, the gift of faith is knowing inside that everything will be as God ordained. When the tunnel is darkest, we see Light. When the river is rising, we know we will not drown.

Very often, the gift of faith is the missing ingredient in our lives. We let the world overtake us when all we have to do is take the gift of faith God has given us and put it into action. We can be overcomers through the gift of faith. Let's let the Holy Spirit give us the gift of faith in the midst of our troubles. He will enable us to march on in victory.

The Gifts of Healings

Definition: The gifts of healings are the supernatural intervention of God restoring wholeness to the sick. Our God is a Healing God. He is still able and willing to heal us of all our diseases (Ps. 103:3).

Notice it is *gifts* of healings, not *gift* of healing. Thirty-nine bloody lashings tore the flesh from Jesus' back on His way to the Cross. It has been said that there are thirty-nine basic diseases from which all sickness arises. That's one lashing for each disease. He endured it all for us!

Jesus said that healing is the children's bread (Mt. 15:21-28). So healing belongs to us. He paid the ultimate price that we might be well and whole. He doesn't bring sickness on us, and He doesn't get the glory from it! He gets glory when we receive His healing.

The Working of Miracles

Definition: The working of miracles is the manifestation of power beyond the natural law of God. It is the divine enablement that you and I can have in impossible situations. With it we can do something that we could not do with natural strength or ability.

A major hurricane was about to strike Virginia Beach. The Christian Broadcasting Network campus would have taken a direct hit, but Pat Robertson took the Word of God and commanded the hurricane to stay out at sea. To the amazement of the weather forecasters and the news media, it veered away from land. CBN was spared. It was a miracle.

We have so much power, but so often it lies dormant in our lives. We could shake this world! But it requires sacrifice. It requires time. It requires giving up the pleasures of life and we don't want to do that!

We too have power with God to avert impending disaster. If we'll pray and speak the Word of God with authority, we too can see good things happen. We can destroy the works of the enemy. Let's just do it!

The Gift of Prophecy

Definition: Prophecy is a divine disclosure in which the Spirit imparts edifying revelation through the spoken word.

1 Cor. 14:3 But he who prophesies speaks edification and exhortation and comfort to men.

Paul stresses that those who operate in this gift must do so with a great deal of care and a heavy sense of responsibility. He clearly states that prophecy provides edification, exhortation, and comfort. In other words, prophecy builds up, encourages, and brings good cheer. In fact, if prophecy tears us down, it is not of God.

Prophecy come from one of three sources: God, the flesh, or the devil. We therefore have a responsibility to judge it. *Despise not prophesying. Hold fast that which is* good (1 Thess. 3:21). So if prophecy doesn't meet the requirements, we are to disregard because it as not coming from the Lord.

Furthermore, if prophecy comes forth in a service, but does not line up with the flow of that service, it is not of God. In addition, if it does not line up with the Bible, then it's not of God. The one who is prophesying also needs to be aware of all of these factors before bringing forth a prophetic word.

Some folks get carried away with personal prophecy. Be careful! If anybody gives you a word of prophecy and it doesn't line up with the word of God, take it with a grain of salt. Say "Thank you," and walk away. It's not necessary to point your finger and say, "You're not of God." Just walk away and pray for that person.

The Gift of Discerning of Spirits

Definition: The gift of discerning of spirits is the ability to see into the spirit world and to understand the circumstances and judge the motives of people.

It's so important to know what is of God and what is not of God, yet so often we just are not aware. An example from my own experience involves speaking in tongues. At times when a person brings forth an utterance in tongues, I have had the Spirit of God alert me, "This is not of Me." I was ministering in a church in Missouri on one occasion when a woman began to speak in tongues. It was disruptive and I had a definite sense that she was not speaking by the Holy Spirit. In that situation, it was necessary to approach her and command that demon to be quiet.

By the gift of discerning of spirits we have knowledge of what is of God and what is not. We have the power and authority in the Name of Jesus to speak to demons and they must obey. There isn't a demon in hell that can overcome us when the Holy Ghost is alive in us with fire.

The Gift of Speaking in Tongues

Acts 2:4 And they were all filled with the Holy Spirit and began to speak with other tongues, as the Spirit gave them utterance.

Definition: The believers were supernaturally speaking languages already known to others although not to the persons speaking.

On the Day of Pentecost, visitors were in Jerusalem from many lands, yet they heard the Gospel being proclaimed in their native tongues by the Spirit-baptized disciples who, in their natural state, could not speak those languages.

In 1 Corinthians 14, Paul talks about another form of speaking in tongues. We refer to it as our *prayer language.* It is for private prayer and worship.

> *1 Cor. 14:14 For if I pray in a tongue, my spirit prays, but my understanding is unfruitful. What is the result then? I will pray with the spirit, and I will also pray with the understanding. I will sing with the spirit, and I will also sing with the understanding.*

Praying in the Spirit doesn't necessarily mean we have to speak in tongues. We can speak in our own language or in tongues when we are praying in the Spirit. When we experience the anointing when we preach, we don't speak in tongues; we speak so that people can clearly understand what we are saying. The anointing sharpens our ability to communicate clearly.

The Gift of Interpretation of Tongues

Definition: The gift of interpretation of tongues is the Spirit-given ability to render a translation of a message first given in tongues. It is not the translation of a foreign language.

On the Day of Pentecost, the believers spoke in tongues but interpretation was neither given nor necessary. On that day, Jesus was reversing the curse of the tower of Babel. There He had brought confusion through disrupting communication by diversifying languages. But here He was bringing unity through reestablishing communication.

We cannot compare the tongue-speaking on the Day of Pentecost with tongue-speaking in the church. It is different, very different.

As <u>He</u> wills

1 Cor. 12:11 But one and the same Spirit works all these things, distributing to each one individually as He wills..

The gifts of the Spirit operate in our lives, not for our good only, but for the good of others. They operate, not as we determine, but as God decides. Our responsibility is to cooperate.

Jesus relied on the Holy Spirit in His earthly ministry the same way that we must. In fact, how much more do we need to rely on the infilling of the Holy Ghost!

Prevailing Power

At the Cross, Jesus deprived Satan of power (Col. 2:13-15). At Pentecost, Jesus made available to us who believe on Him His own disarming, prevailing power over Satan. We have power over every wicked spirit through the shed blood of Christ and the subsequent infilling of the Holy Spirit. In Him, we have power over all the power of the enemy (Lk. 10:19)!

Our Decision

Rom. 11: 29 For the gifts and calling of God are irrevocable.

God has never removed His gifts and callings from the church. God does not take back anything He gives. He doesn't take back our salvation or our healing. He doesn't take back His Holy Spirit. We are the ones who decide if we'll refuse the gifts or if we'll cooperate with the wonderful things the Spirit wants to do in us, through us, and for us.

Fruitful for God

The Holy Spirit fills us in order to impart, not only the power of Christ in us, but also the character of Christ in us.

Gal. 5:22 But the fruit of the Spirit is love, joy, peace, longsuffering, kindness, goodness, faithfulness, gentleness, self-control.

With the Holy Spirit inside us, we will put off the characteristics of flesh. We will take on the traits of our new Spirit person which is joined with the indwelling Holy Spirit. The character of Christ will be seen in us.

The Baptism of the Holy Spirit

The Holy Spirit is present when we are born again, but the Baptism of the Holy Spirit occurs after the new birth. It brings to the outside what God put on the inside of us when we are saved.

We are being changed as we respond to the Holy Spirit in us. We all need to be changed! We all have room to grow more and more into the image of Jesus.

The question is this: Do we want the power of God in our lives? I believe we do! Let's lift our hands to heaven and say, "I want You, Holy Spirit!" Let's pray this prayer together:

Dear Jesus, I need a change in my life. I invite the Holy Spirit to change me, to quicken me, that I will take on the character of Christ. I need Your anointing. Jesus, there are things in my life that do not reflect Your character. From this moment, on I pledge to You that I will look to you for holiness and the fire of the Holy Spirit. I want to change. I want to make a change in my life and in the world around me. Holy Spirit, here I am. Use me. Mold me to the character that will be pleasing to You. Thank you Father for answering prayer.

Chapter 8

Ask. Seek. Knock.

On the Day of Pentecost (Acts 2), the believers who spoke in tongues spoke in known languages. The experience began while they were in prayer in the Upper Room. There the Holy Spirit came to them in a way He had never before come since the beginning of time.

Acts 2:2-4 Suddenly there came a sound from heaven as of a rushing mighty wind and it filled the whole house where they were sitting. Then there appeared to them divided tongues as of fire and one sat upon each of them. They were all filled with the Holy Spirit and began to speak with other tongues as the Spirit gave them utterance.

Just what is *speaking in tongues?* It is an experience of speaking in a language we have never learned. This happens by means of a special ability given to us by the Holy Spirit.

We all speak a language known as our *mother*

tongue. In addition, some people learn a language other than their *mother tongue,* but it is a **learned** language. *Speaking in tongues* is different from both of these because it is a gift given by the Holy Spirit.

Today speaking in tongues is sometimes referred to as *glossolalia.* This term is derived from two Greek words. *Glosso* means *tongue* and *lalein* means *to speak,* so the term means *to speak in/with tongues.*

This experience of speaking in tongues, as it is found in the Bible, is an experience for born again believers only. Anyone can speak gibberish or mimic someone else speaking in tongues. But only those who are filled with the Holy Spirit can speak in tongues in the Biblical sense.

The Sign of the Holy Spirit Baptism

Several passages in Acts besides Chapter 2 indicate that speaking in tongues is the initial sign that a believer has been baptized in the Holy Spirit.

Acts 10:44-46 When Peter was still speaking these words, the Holy Spirit fell upon all of those who heard the word, and those of the circumcision who believed were astonished as many as came with Peter because the gift of the Holy Spirit had been poured out on the Gentiles also for they heard them speak with tongues and magnify God. Then Peter answered, "Can anyone forbid water that these should not be baptized who have received the Holy Spirit just as we have and he commanded them to be baptized in the name of the Lord, then they asked him to stay a few days.

Acts 11:16 John indeed baptized with water, but you shall indeed be baptized in the Holy Spirit.

Acts 15:7 And there had been much dispute, Peter rose up and said to them, "Men and brethren, you know that a good while ago, God chose among us that by my mouth the Gentiles should hear the word of the Gospel and believe, so God who knows the heart acknowledged them by giving the Holy Spirit as he did to us and made no distinction between us purifying the hearts by faith.

Acts 19:6 And when Paul had laid hands on them, the Holy Spirit came upon them and they spoke with tongues and prophesied, and the men were about twelve in all,

What does the evidence of speaking in tongues do for us on a personal level? It is a sign that we have received the Holy Spirit. It is also a sign of the abiding presence of the Holy Spirit in our lives. It is the invigorating, living witness in us who believe. Tongues is an experience that indicates the fullness of the Spirit.

The Old-Time Ways

From the time I was six years old, I grew up in Old-time Pentecost. When we spoke in tongues, we knew we had been baptized in the Holy Spirit! We considered it the Biblical sign that we had received the baptism.

How we sought this wonderful experience! In our zeal, we had certain helps or rituals we observed. Let me share a few of them.

First, we believed in *tarrying*. We earnestly and diligently sought the Lord in prayer for as long as it took to receive. Sometimes it took hours. Other times it took years!

Another common help was to have the seeker repeat certain words and syllables, such as *Jesus*. Eager helpers would urge the seeker to say, "Jesus, Jesus, Jesus." Sooner or later, repeating this faster and faster, the person's tongue would get tired and trip! It worked for some, I guess!

Then there was the habit of several already baptized-in-the-Holy-Ghost believers gathering around the seeker to help the person pray through to the baptism. One person would be shouting, "Hang on! Hang on!" Another would be shouting, "Let go! Let go!" They all meant well! And somehow, people came through speaking in tongues!

We were sincere! But we really don't need to go through these rituals!--or any rituals, for that matter! The Holy Spirit is available instantly to us when we receive Jesus as our Savior and Lord. We simply give ourselves wholly and completely to Him. Just as we received salvation, we receive the gift of the Holy Ghost. We ask Him to baptize us in His Spirit, and we receive our new language as evidence of His gracious gift.

Someone might argue, "I haven't spoken in tongues, so I guess God doesn't want me to!" No, the heavenly language is for everyone who is born again. It is the first sign that we are baptized in the Spirit. This is what happened in the Book of Acts, and this is what happens today.

Who Understands?

When the Spirit was poured out on the Day of Pentecost, Satan knew what the disciples were saying because they spoke in known languages. It is different today because when the Spirit is poured out, we speak in unknown languages. Only God is able to understand these languages. Satan doesn't know what we are saying. It is the Holy Spirit in us helping us to pray in a heavenly language, and God is the only One who understands what we are saying.

The Real Issue: Relationship!

Speaking in tongues does not guarantee that we have Holy Ghost power. To have His power, we must live holy lives. I have heard people say, "Oh, I speak in tongues. I've arrived!" No, speaking in tongues is just the beginning! It's the beginning of an intimate relationship with God through the Holy Spirit, but the fullness of that relationship requires purity on our part.

In Pentecost, we've overemphasized tongues at times! Relationship with God is what it's really all about. It is not so much what comes out of our mouth that matters. It's what is in our heart that counts.

Maybe you have known someone who speaks in tongues, but has a tongue as long as a ski slope! Or maybe you've known someone who speaks in tongues, but is hardly out the church door taking God's Name in vain. I've even known men who speak in tongues in church and beat their wives at home! Speaking in tongues, you see, doesn't make us holy.

Fact or Feeling?

Have you ever heard someone say, "Oh, I can't speak in tongues until I feel it." We may not always feel Him, but He is with us just the same. That's a fact.

For some reason, in Pentecost we think we have to feel a certain way in order to do something for God. "I don't *feel* like singing, so I'm not going to sing!" "I don't *feel* like preaching, so I'm not going to preach." Is it possible that we depend too much on feeling?

Prayer Power

God wants to communicate with us and He wants us to communicate with Him. That is the reason He gives us a personal prayer language.

I suppose my experience in prayer is much like yours. Many times when I start to pray, it seems so hard. I'll say, "Lord, You know what is needed now," and I'll begin to pray in tongues, letting the Spirit take over. When I do this, the lifeless ritual vanishes and my praying is energized by the power of the Spirit!

Prophesied

The gift of tongues was prophesied by the Old Testament prophets and by Jesus Himself. Isaiah 28:11-12 and Joel 2:28-29 foretell it, and in Mark 16:17, Jesus declares His followers would speak in tongues. After the Day of Pentecost, Luke records many occurrences of tongues in the Book of Acts, and Paul writes about the experience especially in his Corinthian letters.

A Big Help!

Speaking in tongues helps us in so many different ways. When we are baptized in the Holy Spirit, speaking in tongues is the first indication of the Holy Spirit's indwelling presence (Acts 2:4). In fact, we cannot be filled with the Holy Spirit and not speak in tongues.

Through this new ability, we receive personal edification from the Spirit living in us, and we also become vessels for public exhortation when the Spirit chooses to give us a message in tongues and interpretation.

A Sign to Unbelievers

1 Cor. 14:22 Therefore tongues are for a sign not to those who believe but to unbelievers.

What does this really mean? Since Paul refers to the Prophet Isaiah in this passage, we should examine what he had to say.

Isaiah 28:11-12 For with stammering lips and another tongue He will speak to this people, To whom He said, "This is the rest with which You may cause the weary to rest," and "This is the refreshing," Yet they would not hear.

The *stammering lips* were the languages of foreign invaders. Their victory over Israel was a sign of divine judgment. It was a warning when they completely rejected what God wanted them to do.

Paul refers to this to say that tongues can be a sign of judgment in the church. It would have the same hardening effect on believers as foreign tongues had on Israel. So we find that it is a sign to the unbeliever because of the hardness of the believers. It was a type of judgment. The response of the unbelievers to the tongue speaking of the believers was that they were out of their minds.

How many times have we had people come to Pentecostal meetings and say, "They are out of their minds! They are crazy. I don't want to go to that church!"

We in Pentecost have been extremists. Once we were overboard on tongues, and now we don't want tongues in the church at all! Sometimes it seems that we don't want any of the gifts operating in the church! We even say the gifts are not necessary. How we need to understand how and when the gifts should be manifested in the church!

Paul speaks plainly from his own experience on these issues. He had to correct problems with the zealous Corinthians. Paul had no problem with gifts being in operation, but he had to help the Corinthians use the gifts correctly. Let's learn from Paul and from our own experience.

Chapter 9

Direct Line

The baptism of the Holy Spirit gives us a direct link with God. It enables us to have an intimate relationship with Him. It provides an atmosphere for the gifts and fruit of the Spirit to grow. It helps us to be more sensitive to others so that we can minister as Jesus would.

What a mistake it is to think that we are baptized in the Spirit so that we can walk down the street speaking in tongues! Some folks mistakenly think that is how we show we are not ashamed of the Gospel. They mean well, but they are not helping anybody, especially the people who need to get saved. In fact, it makes people think we are crazy. They just walk away shaking their heads in bewilderment. We want to win the lost, not draw attention to ourselves!

Nevertheless, speaking in tongues is a gift that every believer should have the joy of experiencing. Paul expresses this in his advice to the Corinthian church.

1 Cor. 14:5 I wish you all spoke with tongues. More than that that you prophecy for he who prophecies is greater than he who speaks in tongues unless indeed he interprets that the church may receive edification.

If we are baptized in the Holy Spirit, we have our prayer language, but we do not all have the gift of tongues and interpretation. So Paul tells us not to speak in tongues in the congregation unless the one speaking or someone else present is gifted to bring the interpretation. Since the purpose of tongues is the edification of the congregation, a message without interpretation cannot fulfil its purpose. Tongues in the congregation requires interpretation, then. That's one way we know that tongues without interpretation is for personal edification only.

Have you ever been in a service when someone gave a message in tongues and no interpretation followed? Perhaps the person was young in the things of the Lord and did not understand his or her responsibility. Or perhaps the one with the interpretation was disobedient in not bringing forth that interpretation. Or perhaps the message in tongues was simply for personal edification and not intended by the Lord for public expression. Regardless, when this happens, everyone waits and waits and waits for the interpretation and after while the Spirit is quenched. In a situation like this, I just begin to sing and worship God so that the Holy Spirit continues to flow and no one becomes uneasy.

Blessings begin to fall when people are able to receive what the Spirit is saying through the gifts of prophecy and tongues and interpretation. In the congregation, these gifts normally reinforce the theme of the preacher's message. When the Spirit flows through these gifts, He will exhort, lift up, and bring comfort.

We've Had Some Strange Ideas!

In Pentecostal circles at least, when we can say we have spoken in tongues, we've thought we had arrived! We've had some strange ideas! The truth is, if we don't demonstrate the fruit of the Spirit in our lives, we probably should ask, "What good is tongues?"

Another of our strange ideas is that if we don't speak in tongues we won't make it to heaven. At least that's what I was taught growing up in Pentecost. Some Pentecostal folks still believe that way. They even refuse to fellowship with believers who don't speak in tongues. What a shock awaits them in heaven! There they will have to get along with Baptists, Presbyterians,

Methodists, Catholics, and all blood-washed believers, some who speak in tongues and some who don't. Jesus told Nicodemus that the way to Heaven is to be born again (Jn. 3:1-21).

An attitude we must repent of is pride mixed with ignorance. Is it possible that we Pentecostals have used the gift of tongues to glorify self instead of God? Have we been proud of our gift instead of God? Have we used it to boast, "I'm a tongue-talking, Holy Roller!"

All of this is not to say that speaking in tongues is not important. It is vital that we use our prayer language everyday because it builds us up on the inside, but I also believe that we need more than tongues. We need a genuine relationship with Jesus Christ. We need to walk in the Holy Spirit, obedient to His will and developing the fruit of the Spirit in daily life.

The Real *Versus* the Counterfeit

Perhaps one problem we Pentecostals have is that we haven't always discerned between Satan's counterfeit gifts and the genuine gifts of the Holy Spirit. We need to listen carefully to the Holy Spirit inside us. For example, at times when I have heard people speak in tongues, I have known instantly in my spirit that it was not of God. Jesus would speak and say, "This is not of Me."

Why *Tongues?*

The Bible describes two basic purposes of speaking in tongues. One is for personal edification and the other is for public exhortation. The main thing to remember is that in both cases, according to Acts 2:4, it is the Holy Spirit who gives the utterance.

Acts 2:4 And they were all filled with the Holy Spirit and began to speak with other tongues, as the Spirit gave them utterance.

Paul's Instructions Concerning the Gifts

Paul gave clear instructions about the operation of the gifts. In 1 Corinthians 12-14, he gives us insight and direction. Chapter 14 is especially helpful concerning practical aspects of the gifts.

1 Cor. 14:2

1 Cor. 14:2 For he who speaks in a tongue does not speak to men but to God, for no one understands him, however, in the spirit he speaks mysteries, but he who prophesies speaks edification, exhortation, and comfort to men.

He who speaks in a tongue edifies himself but he who prophesies edifies the church.

What is Paul saying here? He is simply stating that speaking in tongues is a private matter and its purpose is spiritual self-edification. It is intended for personal prayer and praise to God. Does that mean that we cannot praise God in tongues and use our prayer language at church? No. It means that we need to understand how to operate in the gift.

Paul indicates that the prayer language does have a place during praise and worship when there are no unbelievers or uninformed people present. God has blessed us with this gift and He expects us to use it, but He expects us to exercise wisdom in its use. It's really a matter of common sense.

Are we guilty of sometimes becoming so emotionally involved in our religious experience that we forget to love the people around us? Suppose we were to sit beside someone who doesn't understand about speaking in tongues. Our first responsibility would be to be sensitive to that person so as not to frighten him or her away from church and away from the Lord.

In 1 Cor. 14:2, Paul is not talking about the tongues that were given on the Day of Pentecost. On the Day of Pentecost the disciples spoke in known languages understood by people and by Satan. In this case, Paul is speaking of our heavenly language or the unknown tongue that only God and our spirit understand. He tells us that this kind of speaking in tongues is directed to God, not people.

1 Cor. 14:3-4

1 Cor. 14:3-4 But he who prophecies speaks edification and exhortation and comfort to men. He who speaks in a tongue edifies himself but he who prophesies edifies the church.

Paul says that speaking in tongues is a precious gift to be used with a sense of responsibility. It is not to be used for show or to make us feel important in front of other people. It is a private gift for our personal edification. It is a gift from God that empowers our prayers and our praise. It can also be helpful in open worship services. Paul advises us not to speak in tongues out loud if there are people present who do not understand the operation of this gift.

1 Cor. 14:5

In 1 Cor. 14:5, Paul says he wishes we all spoke with tongues, but he says it is better that we prophesy. If the preacher were to stand before the congregation and speak in tongues, no one would know what was being said. Before long the congregation would say, "I wish the preacher would speak in English! I can't understand what's being said, and I'm not getting anything out of this!"

Paul goes on to say that if we do speak in tongues, interpretation must follow. Many times we have heard tongues come forth in a service with no interpretation. Perhaps no one present had the gift of interpretation, or maybe the tongues was personal praise to God. In that case it should have been done quietly in a manner that would not have disturbed the service. We all may have our prayer language, but not all have tongues and interpretation.

The gifts of prophecy and speaking in tongues with interpretation come forth under the anointing of the Holy Spirit, and not as we choose. On the other hand, we can speak in our prayer language any time because the Holy Spirit lives inside us. I have heard people say, "I can't speak in tongues unless I get a special anointing from God." But each of us who is baptized in the Holy Spirit has been given *the anointing that abides within* so that whenever we pray, we can pray in our prayer language.

Speaking in tongues is a wonderful gift, but perhaps we have stressed it too much. We have thought that we must give a message in tongues in every service, but that is not so. A message is to come forth only as the Holy Spirit prompts. Our responsibility is to be available to the Holy Spirit, to be holy vessels through whom He can work. It is the Holy Spirit's responsibility to provide the utterance. We simply respond.

1 Cor. 14:6

In verse 6, Paul stresses the fact that tongues must be interpreted. He reminds us that it is better to explain a revelation, a knowledge, or a teaching in the tongue that everybody understands than to speak in tongues that no one understands.

1 Cor. 14:7-9

In these verses, Paul notes that clear instructions are important generally in life, and that this is especially true in relating the things of God. We all need the knowledge and wisdom that comes from God, so we cannot afford to be carried off into some kind of emotional frenzy as has happened so much in Pentecost.

In over forty years in Pentecost, I've seen too much fanaticism. I've seen people dance right across the tops of the pews! I believe in dancing before God, but let's not get carried away to where we are no earthly good. Let's take that energy and pray for somebody who is in the midst of a deep trial, or let's lay hands on somebody who needs the infilling of the Holy Ghost. I like nothing more than a good Pentecostal service, but we must know how to channel all that Holy Ghost energy for the benefit of individuals and for the good of the congregation.

Paul continues to give guidelines. Although he is dealing specifically with problems of misdirected zeal and sins of immorality in the Corinthian church, he is also speaking to us today. He calls for repentance in lifestyle and for a more orderly use of the gifts of the Spirit, including the gift of tongues.

1 Cor. 14:10-13

In verses 10-13, Paul tells us that the best gift is prophecy. By this, he is not belittling the gifts of tongues and interpretation. He is simply pointing out again the importance of the listeners being able to profit from the utterance, and that is possible only if it is in a language they understand. So speaking in tongues by itself is not the best gift, but when it is accompanied by interpretation it has the same effect as prophecy.

1 Cor. 14:14

In verse 14, he reminds us that praying in tongues is praying in the Spirit. When we pray in the Spirit, we don't understand what we are praying. We know that the Holy Spirit is praying on our behalf according to the will of God, but we don't know what is being said.

Another thing to be aware of is that it is not necessary to speak in tongues to be praying in the Spirit. We can worship God in the Spirit or be in the midst of a move of the Holy Spirit, but not speak in tongues. We can pray in the Spirit and yet understand what we are praying because we are using our native language.

1 Cor. 14:15-19

In verses 15-19, Paul discusses speaking in a heavenly language. He was a brilliant person who also spoke in other languages of his day. Yet he said, *In the church I would rather speak five words with my understanding, that I may teach others also, than ten thousand words in a tongue.*

If we could understand Paul's approach, it would help us today. Paul is so consumed with the need to help people grow in spiritual things, but we seem to be more concerned about looking spiritual. We go to church saying, "O God, let me speak in tongues. Let me give a message.

O Lord, let me give a prophecy." Then we sit there and begin to speak in tongues in the middle of the service and we disturb everyone. Some people don't know what is going on and they say, "I'm not going to sit beside that person again!" Or they just don't come back to church.

Paul doesn't clearly say, "Don't use your prayer language in church." Nor does he say, "Use your prayer language in church." He just gives some guidelines, perhaps because in His day the believers did not meet in church buildings, and the meetings were believers' meetings. Today, we have a different situation and we need to be sensitive to those who come into our midst who are not aware of the gifts of the Spirit.

Basically, what Paul tells us is this: Praying in tongues is for personal use and is for personal edification. Speaking in tongues or giving a message in church is to edify the church and must be accompanied by interpretation.

One thing Paul does make clear in this whole discussion is that we should be obedient to the leadership of the church. If we go into a church that doesn't practice speaking in tongues, then we should not stand up and speak in tongues because it would be disrespectful. Our actions could tear that church apart, so Paul encourages us to do everything in decency and order.

Now, if we enter a Pentecostal church, we have an entirely different situation. We presume that the leadership believes in the gifts, so we are free to worship and praise openly. We can bring forth a message in tongues and interpretation, or we can bring forth a prophetic word. Whatever God lays on our heart, in that situation, we are free to obey.

1 Cor. 14:20

In verse 20, Paul warns us to be innocent as children when it comes to evil, but to be mature when it comes to godliness. We are to grow up! It is so vital that we be people of intelligence who know how to deal wisely in all the affairs of life. It is so important that we have knowledge and correct understanding of the God's Word.

1 Cor. 14:21-26

In verses 21-26, Paul's explains that there is a time for tongues, interpretation, and prophecy in our worship services. God doesn't prompt a person to interrupt the person preaching, but He does impart wisdom about when and how to minister the gift to the congregation.

Some folks will argue, "But if we have to wait, we'll quench the Spirit. We must give it when it comes." On the other hand, the Bible tells us that *the spirit of the prophet is subject to the prophet* (1 Cor. 14:32). It tells us that we are responsible to operate in the gifts of the Spirit in decency and in order (1 Cor. 14:40).

1 Cor. 14:27

In verse 27, Paul instructs us to bring only two or three messages in a service. This directive is not always followed. There are well meaning people who think they need to be heard to be considered spiritual. When ten or twelve messages in tongues and interpretations come forth, it gets boring! People get restless and no one is edified except the person giving the message. God is the Great Communicator, and He is able to speak clearly and concisely.

1 Cor. 14:28

In verse 28, Paul instructs us concerning interpretation. If there is no one present with the gift of interpretation, we should not bring forth a message in tongues. Another option is that the one bringing the message should pray to receive the interpretation. If an interpreter is not present and if we have not been gifted to interpret, it is best to refrain from bringing forth the message in tongues. It is best to be quiet and to talk to the Lord about it. Many times in these situations we are simply speaking in our prayer language and we should not disrupt the congregation.

1 Cor. 14:29

In verse 29, Paul tells us that if a prophecy comes forth, we have the responsibility to judge or evaluate it. Is it of God? Does it agree with the Bible? Is it pertinent to what is going on in the service?

1 Cor. 14:30-31

Verse 30 brings to mind another difficult situation that occurs from time to time. Sometimes when one person begins to give a message in tongues, all of a sudden, someone else jumps up over here and another over there, and all three are trying to give their messages. Confusion reigns! Paul's advice concerning such a dilemma is for the first person to fall silent. He says that everyone can take a turn. That way everyone can hear and be encouraged.

1 Cor. 14:32

In verse 32, Paul tells us that when the Holy Spirit deposits a gift in us, we become responsible for that gift. It simply means, for example, that we are to bring a message in tongues at the right time and in an orderly fashion. Doing this does not quench the Spirit. If the Lord has given us a message in tongues, it will still be there when the appropriate time comes to bring it forth. God does not give it to us and then take it away if we cannot give it immediately.

1 Cor. 14:33-35

In verse 33, Paul declares that God doesn't like disorder, disharmony, or confusion. He likes harmony, and so Paul instructs the Corinthians to walk in harmony and peace.

He also gives instructions in verses 34-36 regarding the women of that day who, under paganism had been kept in ignorance and bondage. Now as Christians, they had new freedom and dignity, but they had to grow in understanding. To keep peace and order in public gatherings, Paul recommended that their husbands answer their questions at home. He was concerned with peace and order in the services, and so he was giving directives that would alleviate disruptive behavior. Speaking in tongues was not wrong, and women asking questions was not wrong, but Paul was advising the Corinthians on the best and least disruptive approach.

1 Cor. 14:36-38

In verse 36-38, Paul seems to be encouraging the Corinthians to take seriously what he is saying. Even the most esteemed prophets and those who considered themselves prophets were to recognize their need of instruction. Those who refused to learn are responsible for the consequences of their ignorance.

1 Cor. 14:39-40

In verses 39-40, Paul did not want the Corinthians to stop using the gifts. In the same way today, we are not to quench the Spirit by not using the gifts. By God's grace, we can follow Paul's instructions and press into the deepest anointings from the throne of God.

Chapter 10

Knowing the Future

The popular use of the term *charismatic* originated with a Lutheran preacher a few years ago when the gifts of the Spirit began occurring among Lutherans. He tagged it the renewal of the *charismatic* or spiritual gifts. That term caught on and the general renewal in the denominational churches became known as the *Charismatic Renewal.*

When the Charismatic Renewal began to sweep the nation and the world, the Pentecostals took a back seat about the spiritual gifts. The truth is that before the Charismatic Renewal broke out we had already taken a back seat regarding the spiritual gifts. But with this great movement of the Spirit, we tended to react critically and fearfully. Consequently most Pentecostals decided not to get involved. Whether we realize it or not, what we were really saying was this: "Let's not stir up the spiritual gifts. It's better that they don't operate."

We Pentecostals suddenly found ourselves on the other end of the scale regarding the spiritual gifts. Whereas we had once encouraged the operation of the gifts, we now reacted against them! Could we not find the happy medium? Recently, we've become more open, and the term *Pentecostal* is again becoming popular among Spirit-baptized believers.

What Really Matters?

It really doesn't matter what terminology we use. It doesn't matter if we call the gifts *spiritual* gifts or *charismatic* gifts.

What does matter is the origin of these gifts. Do they originate with God? With self? Or the Devil?

Does all prophecy, for example, come from God? No, all prophecy does not come from God. Some comes from self, and some even comes from the Devil.

Another thing that matters is when and how we use the gifts. For example, the question has been asked: "When should the gift of prophecy be exercised in the service?" One of the best times to bring forth a prophecy is during open praise time. Probably the wrong times are during the offering and the sermon. You see, God does not interrupt the anointed message. If there is a word of prophecy to be brought forth, it can be brought before or after the sermon. If God wants a prophetic word to be brought forth during the preaching, He speaks to the preacher who then pauses in anticipation of the message.

We must understand that God is a God of decency and order. He is not the author of confusion! He does not prompt us to interrupt a preacher with a prophetic word. Neither does He put on a show! Furthermore, He does not intend for His gifts to be used for entertainment! Nor does He intend them to be used to tear people down. He gives us gifts to edify, exhort and comfort others and to bring praise to Him.

I still remember when I first went to a Pentecostal church and heard the gifts operating in the church. It was a very strong Pentecostal church and the gifts operated on a very high level. Although I was only six years old, I was aware that God was working supernaturally in our midst.

Test Everything All the Time!

How we all love to receive a prophetic word! In our excitement, however, we must remember to test or judge what comes forth. It doesn't matter who gives it! According to the Bible, every prophetic word must be tested.

1 Thess. 5:20-21   Do not despise prophecies. Test all things; hold fast what is good.

So we are to judge every prophetic word. That means we are to evaluate it and decide if it is from God and if it is actually for us. We can ask, "Does this pertain to me? Is this really what God is saying to me?"

Christians are not the only ones who like a supernatural directive. The people of the world love it! They're spending more and more money today on ouija boards, fortune tellers, and palm readers. The psychic networks are flourishing! Everyone wants to know what the future holds for them! It seems to be a part of human nature!

My suggestion is to go to the Word of God. Yes, go to the Word of God. It is our sure word of prophecy.

According to 1 Cor. 12:4-11, the gifts of the Spirit come from the Spirit of God by the will of God. They do not come by the will of men and women. They are not the property of this or that denomination. They come forth by the will and power of the Holy Spirit.

This is why the true gift of prophecy is spontaneous. It's not something we work up, although some people approach it that way! They rehearse what they are going to say in order to make sure it will sound good. Prophecy that originates with the Holy Spirit will be unrehearsed and spontaneous.

Thus Sayeth the Lord . . .

We've all heard the phrase *thus sayeth the Lord.* We've probably all used it at some time, either when we operate in a spiritual gift or when we are just sharing with others. A word of caution is in order here. Let's be sure it really is of the Lord! Let's not be deluded or careless in attributing to God what is really only of self or perhaps even of Satan. Don't blame **God** for something **you** want to say!

Sometimes God really does speak to us. This is accompanied by great joy. Other times we sense the Lord giving us specific information not related to our own lives, information of which we would otherwise have no knowledge.

For much of what we need to know, we can and should go to the Bible. It is God's Word to us. I've heard people say, "If God wants me to go and do this or that, then He will speak to me through somebody. If God wants me to be a witness, then He will give me a word through someone." No, the Bible has already told us we are to be witnesses. We don't need an additional directive about this.

Prophecy Reinforces
What God Has Already Told Us.

We must be careful in giving personal words. Somebody might look at someone else and say, "God has called you to be a preacher." Oh, it sounds great, but did God really call that person to be a preacher? It is so dangerous for a person to take it upon self to call a person into the ministry! If they go, they will probably fail because it wasn't God who called them and so they didn't have His anointing on their ministry.

A personal prophecy, you see, will reinforce what God has already been saying to that person in private. For example, when God called me to be a preacher, it was so real I didn't need anybody to give me a prophetic word. It happened thirty years ago when I was lying in a hospital bed recovering from a severe accident. It was one of the worst accidents in many years in western Pennsylvania.

I was able to share this story one day with a man who had come to inspect our carpet. I discovered that both his father and grandfather had been Church of God preachers. He said, "I've been a Catholic and I've been divorced six years. I say my prayers every night, but I know I'm not where I need to be with God. How did you know when God called you to be a preacher?"

I was able to share with him how God said to me, "You are to take My message and win the lost." That was the call that came upon me that day in the hospital when I was unable even to move out of bed. God gave me the call.

Prophecy must be tested and carefully delivered or it can bring confusion and trouble. It is never God's will to confuse or trouble anyone with the gifts. Our lives are precious to God.

When we operate in any gift, it must be with the anointing of the Holy Spirit. We are to be thankful, but not puffed up when the Lord uses us to bless others!

One Terrible Revival!

I like nothing more than to let prophecy or tongues and interpretations come forth, but it must be done in the anointing of the Holy Spirit. With that anointing there will be Holy Ghost order. I remember one incident where we were evangelizing in a little country church, and there was no order of any kind. In fact there was sheer confusion, it seemed, about everything.

When they got up to sing, they all sang in their own key and they all had their own beat. The instruments were the same way. My daughter said to the preacher's daughter, "Tell me, what key do you all play in?" She said, "Daddy said we don't have to play in any key. He says 'Just hit it, Daughter! Hit it and let it go!'"

When I got up to pray for the sick, all I had to do was walk toward them and they would fall out underneath the pews. There were blankets stashed under the front pew ready and waiting to cover them when they fell!

Now, if somebody falls out before God, that's fine, as long as it's God! Believe me, I've experienced it and I know when it's God, but I've seen some go down when it's not God doing it! We can't afford to have a circus going on in the altar service! God isn't pleased with that sort of thing!

God wants to minister. He wants to heal the sick and set the captives free, but when folks put on a show, God's true work is hindered. On the other hand, nothing is so beautiful to see as a person slain in the Spirit and come up a renewed believer or a new creature in Christ Jesus.

In another revival, I saw a young man come down for salvation. He said, "I want to be saved." I asked, "Are you ready to say the sinner's prayer?" He said, "Yes." I proceeded to lay hands on him and lead him in the sinner's prayer, and when I came to the name of Jesus, he began to speak in tongues. But my spirit did not witness with his spirit, and God said to me, "This is not of Me." At the same time that I could feel the holy anointing arising in me, I saw this man begin to come up as a vulture. First he came toward me but then he turned quickly and headed for a boy, the preacher's son, who was sitting on the front pew. I was about to restrain him when the Holy Spirit directed me to touch his forehead. Immediately the man fell to the floor. The Spirit of God dealt with him and when he finally stood up, he was a new creature in God. He was not like a vulture any more. No longer was he speaking in the tongues of a demon. Instead he was praising and glorifying God! Hallelujah!

The revival as a whole was a terrible experience! I couldn't wait to get out of town! What a tragedy it is to see a body of believers with no training and no discipline. One of a pastor's main jobs is to teach and train the believers.

Decency and Order

1 Cor. 14:40 Let all things be done decently and in order.

From Paul's letter to the Corinthians, we can see how disorderly the Corinthian church was! What was true of the Corinthians is too often true today. It's time for all of us to move with the Holy Spirit in decency and order.

But let's be careful in our quest for decency and order not to quench the Spirit and not to despise prophecy. Paul counsels us along these lines in his letter to the Thessalonians, when he writes, *Do not quench the Spirit. Do not despise prophecy (1 Thess. 5:19).* He goes on to warn us:

1 Thess 5:21 Test all things; hold fast what is good. Abstain from every form of evil.

Notice the link here between evil and disorderly conduct. One important means of refraining from evil, according to Paul, is to walk decently and in order. We think that verse refers only to the sins of the world, but that is not what it says. It tells us to abstain from *every form of evil*. That includes disorderly conduct in spiritual things.

This verse indicates that the Thessalonian church was guilty of quenching the Spirit in some other manner. We think we are *quenching the Spirit* when we don't run, shout, or operate in the gifts of the Spirit. That's not what this verse means. Instead it has to do with *dampening the flame* of the Holy Spirit.

Consider John the Baptist's words:

Lk. 3:16. John answered, saying to them all, "I indeed baptize you with water; but One mightier than I is coming, whose sandal strap I am not worthy to loose. he will baptize you with the Holy Spirit and with fire.

What is this *fire* spoken of by John the Baptist? It is that which purifies us. The Spirit empowers us and the fire purifies us. How many of us seem to want the power but not the purging!?

Fire also refers to that aspect of the Holy Spirit's work in us that enlightens, warms, and consumes. So Paul warns us *not to quench the Spirit. (1 Thess. 5:19)*. We are to be careful not to quench the fire of the Spirit. *Quenching* is a refusal to allow the Holy Spirit to flow into our bodies to cleanse us from the sins of the earth. It results in the state we jokingly refer to as being God's *frozen chosen.*

Are we God's *frozen chosen?* Do we believe God would have us be staid and sedate!

On the other hand, maybe some of us go to the other extreme. We disrupt others with our exaggerated response to God? In other words, we want the emotional high we experience in God's presence, yet we still want to live in sin! We want to come to church and run around the house. We want to jump the pews. We want to fall out before God. But that's all we want. We don't want the purifying fire of the Holy Spirit.

Despising Prophecy

Another way that we can quench the Spirit is by despising God's prophetic messages. If a prophetic word is from God, it should be allowed. We should never hinder it by cynicism or suspicion. These attitudes hinder the genuine work of the Holy Spirit.

The prophetic gift has been so mishandled that many Pentecostals have rejected the gift altogether. But God is still speaking through the prophetic gift. We must receive it and allow the blessing to flow. The church needs the prophetic gift operating in the midst of the congregation.

The prophetic gift was important in both the Old and New Testaments. In Samuel 12:1-15, for example, the prophet Nathan exercised the gift in exposing David's sin. In Acts 13: 1-3, the prophetic word came to Paul and Barnabus to give direction to their first missionary journey.

What Prophecy Does

1 Cor. 14:3 But he who prophesies speaks edification, exhortation and comfort to man.

Notice the purpose of prophecy. It is to edify or build up. It is to exhort, warn or counsel. It is to comfort or encourage. But it is never to beat down or condemn. Yet how many times we have heard it abused in this way. The spirit of prophecy is the Spirit of Jesus, and Jesus came, not to condemn the world, but to save it. If we bring forth a prophetic word that causes suffering or shame, the blood is on our hands.

Judging Prophecy

1 Cor. 14:29. Let two or more speak and let the others judge.

We have to be willing to judge prophecy. The human vessel is not a perfect delivery system, and static of various kinds can distort the message. Perhaps, for example, some people enjoy the limelight too much and operate in the gifts to be important. Others may not be walking with God, yet they think they can still prophecy. This is not true, of course, because the prophetic word is to be an outgrowth of our relationship with God.

The Bible calls this judging of prophecy *testing the spirits*. We are to judge whether or not a prophecy is of the Lord. There are guidelines to help us.

- **Does the message line up with God's written word?** If the message given deviates from the principles of Scripture, then it must be rejected. Prophecy must not be the fruit of own thoughts.

- **Does the message confirm previously revealed direction from God?** In the case of Paul and Barnabus, the prophetic message provided guidance for the mission already established in their hearts. God informs us **first** of His will and prophecy simply confirms what God has already said to us. It's **never** the other way around. We should never change jobs or marry based solely on a prophetic word. God never intended His prophetic message to be His initial or final line of communication. He lives within each of us by His Spirit and wants to communicate directly with each of us.

We live in a day when it seems that everybody wants a prophetic word. Everybody wants to know something from God. We can experience this by spending quality time with God in His Word and in prayer. The Bible makes it clear that God's children are led by the Holy Spirit, not by personal prophecies.

Rom. 8:14. For as many as have been led by the Spirit of God, these are the sons of God.

The person who lives according to the flesh will die spiritually. To be led by the Spirit is to put to death the deeds of the body and live. The Holy Spirit will never lead us into action contrary to the Scriptures. But that's what a lot of these so-called prophetic messages are encouraging today. They have very active imaginations!

Oh, how our churches need to be alive with the Holy Spirit! How the Pentecostal church needs to get back to flowing in the charismatic gifts! But let's not make it a circus. Instead let's do it God's way.

Chapter 11

Super Victorious

Real faith in God puts us over in life. *The just,* the Bible says, *shall live by faith* (Hab. 2:4; Rom. 1:17; Heb. 10:38), and without faith, we cannot please God (Heb. 11:6). So faith is important.

There are different kinds of faith. It can be either natural faith or supernatural faith. Natural faith is a quality we all possess. Supernatural faith, on the other hand, comes from the Holy Spirit. This is the faith we need to please God.

Natural Faith

We exercise natural faith everyday without thinking about it. For example, we sit on a chair without fear of it collapsing. We drive on hazardous freeways believing that we'll arrive safely at our destination. It takes faith!

Another example of natural faith is the farmer who plants seed expecting a harvest. He puts seeds of corn in the ground believing that they will spring up and produce more corn. If the farmer didn't have faith, he wouldn't plant the seed. He would eat it instead. He plants that seed because he has natural faith.

Supernatural Faith

Supernatural faith comes from God. It may be in the form of saving faith or the gift of faith. It is the ability to believe God now in the face of impossibility. It is the ability to combat unbelief with inner conviction, with a very real sense of knowing that it is birthed in us by the Spirit. It is the ability to meet adverse circumstances with trust in Christ and His words. Supernatural faith makes us super victorious.

Spiritual Strength

Romans 1:11 For I long to see you that I may impart to you some spiritual gift, so you may be established.

Paul longed to visit the believers in Rome. He wanted to see them flourish and he knew that they would if the Spirit and the gifts were welcome in their midst. He knew they would be a super victorious church.

Today in the church, we have the same need as the church of Rome in Paul's day. We need to stir up the spiritual gifts. Oh, we have lots of excuses why the gifts shouldn't operate! Many churches have completely pushed out the Spirit and His gifts. Because of this, the church is weak and homes are disrupted by trouble of all kinds.

What Is a *Spiritual Gift?*

The term *spiritual gift* comes from the Greek word *charisma*. Paul uses this term in writing to the Romans and the Corinthians.

Rom. 12:6 Having then gifts differing according to the grace that is given to us, let us use them.

1 Cor. 12:1 Now concerning spiritual gifts, brethren, I do not want you to be ignorant.

In this verse, the literal translation is *spirituals* rather than *spiritual gifts*. Paul's use of *spirituals* rather than *gifts* shows his focus on the Source of the power, rather than on the power itself.

One of the *spirituals* Paul talks about in 1 Corinthians 12 is the gift of faith.

1 Cor. 12:7 But the manifestation of the

Spirit is given to each one for the profit of all . . . to another faith by the same Spirit. . . .

He explains that the gift of faith and all the gifts are given by the Holy Spirit.

Not every redeemed person has the gift of faith in operation. Everyone should, but not everyone does! Everyone has the gift of faith because it resides in the indwelling Holy Spirit, but we must learn to release it.

Saving Faith

Saving faith accompanies the preaching of the Gospel. When a person hears the Gospel, that person must either accept Jesus by faith and be saved or reject Jesus and be lost. Everyone who has received Jesus as Savior and Lord has this saving faith.

An example of this saving faith is found in Luke 23:42. Here the thief dying on a cross beside Jesus when Jesus Himself was being crucified, expressed saving faith.

Lk. 23:42-43 He said to Jesus, "Lord, remember me when you come into your kingdom. And Jesus said to him, "Assuredly, I say to you, today you will be with Me in Paradise."

Another example of saving faith is found in Acts 16:16-34 in the story of Paul and Silas in the Philippian jail.

Acts 16:25-30 But at midnight Paul and Silas were praying and singing hymns to God and the prisoners were listening to them. Suddenly there was a great earthquake, so that the foundations of the prison were shaken and immediately all the doors were opened and everyone's chains were loosed. And the keeper of the prison, awakening from sleep and seeing the prison doors open, supposing the prisoners had fled, drew his sword and was about to kill himself. But Paul called with a loud voice saying, "Do yourself no harm, for we are all here." Then he called for a light, ran in, and fell down trembling before Paul and Silas. And he brought them out and said, "Sirs, what must I do to be saved?" So they said, "Believe on the Lord Jesus Christ, and you will be saved, you and your household."

This is the faith we need to be converted. It is the kind of faith that says, "Yes, I believe Jesus is my Savior." This is the kind of faith we need when we're sick and we don't know what to do. It's the kind of faith we need to overcome financial problems. It is the saving, delivering power of faith at work in us who believe.

Sometimes we make excuses for ourselves. We

think that Paul was different from us. No! He was as human and subject to pain and trouble as we are. Do we really understand that Paul was in prison praising God when this spectacular display of supernatural power occurred?

At some time, we all have to stand against trouble or sickness or heartache that seems greater than we can bear. It's then that we must choose to praise God. It's then that we must resist the devil and his attacks. It's then that our praise releases the tangible anointing of the Holy Spirit.

It's when it seems that all hell is arraigned against us that we must look to God who is faithful in everything in every way all the time. It's then that we must hold forth God's Word of truth against the trial. If we are attacked with sickness, we speak God's Word of healing and claim health. You see, we are the set-free ones! We are the victorious ones in Him! We are the ones whom God has appointed to take His Word to this world.

The Gift of Faith

Why can't we operate in the gift of faith with the same ease that we do with natural faith? The reason is that the gift of faith is different from other types of faith. The gift of faith is faith that comes with the anointing of the Holy Spirit. It is special faith that supernaturally achieves what is impossible through human effort. It flows from the Spirit. It is not worked up. We can do nothing to enhance it. All we do is believe and receive. It is the faith of Jesus, the faith that worked and that still works in and through Him.

Let's consider an example in the life of Jesus.

*Lk. 8:22 Now it happened on a certain day, that He got into a boat with His disciples. And He said to them, "Let us go over to the other side of the lake." And they launched out. But as they sailed He fell asleep. And a windstorm came down on the lake, and they were filling with water, and were in jeopardy. And they came to Him and awoke Him, saying, "Master, Master, we are perishing!" And He arose and rebuked the wind and the raging of the water. And they ceased, and there was a calm. But He said to them, **"Where is your faith?"** And they were afraid, and they marveled, saying one to another, "Who can this be? For he commands even the winds and water, and they obey Him!"*

When Jesus commanded the tempest to be stop, the sea immediately became calm. This was the result of faith. All Jesus did was speak the word of faith. He said, "Be still."

We too have the power to still life's storms. We have the power to rebuke the Devil and his demons that are trying to destroy our homes, our churches, and our nation. We have this power available to us, but we have to learn to let the gift of faith rise up in us to overpower the storms.

We drink from the same fountain from which Jesus drank. This fountain never runs dry. We have the same power flowing through us that flowed through Him. We have the same strength, the same wisdom, the same knowledge, and the same anointing of the Holy Spirit. We have the power of God working in us and through us to crush all adversity.

We can't do it in our frail humanity, but God can and will if we'll only cooperate with Him. God is the Only Source, and He is the Giver of the gift of faith.

More than Conquerors!

Rom. 8:37 Yet in all these things we are more than conquerors through Him who loved us.

The gift of faith makes us conquerors. Yes!

But it makes us more than conquerors through Him who loves us. We are not just victorious. We are super victorious through Christ.

We don't have to be weak, sick, defeated Christians. We are to be winners. Through Christ, we can overcome every work of the enemy and live in victory, peace, and abundance.

It's great to be a winner! It's better to be more than a winner! Some folks are happy to win one here and another there, and be defeated the rest of the time. No! We are to live as overcomers all the time through the power of the Holy Spirit at work in us, for us, and through us.

To Win or Not to Win?

This victory is not automatic. Always we have the responsibility to choose between victory and defeat. By our choice, we give room either to the destructive work of darkness or to the wonderful works of God. We can dwell on the problems and complain all day long, or we can remind ourselves of God's Word and speak it with confidence.

It's not conceit to speak our victories. It honors God. It magnifies His greatness. It is an expression of confidence in Him.

Victory doesn't come when we're complaining. It comes when we are laying hold of it by fighting the good fight of faith, knowing that God is on our side. When we exercise this kind of faith, the gift of faith, we release the power of God to work on our behalf.

That is what happened for Paul and Silas in prison. They exercised faith and God did the rest. They did their part and God did His! They praised God and He brought a victory. It was far beyond anything they could have achieved on their own. It was sensational.

A Sensational, Supernatural Church

The world today needs to see a supernatural church. They need to see the sensational power of God at work in the midst of believers. Would you want to attend a church that's dead, cold, and indifferent? No! We need a spectacular move of the Spirit of God in our midst!

We need to break loose of our doubts and fears. We need to rise above circumstances by the power of God. Paul and Silas rose above their desperate conditions in jail. We're not in jail! But how often do we act as though we are bound by chains and held captive behind the bars of adversity? We're not in jail. We're free.

God has done what needs to be done for our

victory. He continues to manifest victory on our behalf if we'll just let Him. We can have the power of God operating in our lives.

That doesn't mean we can be nonchalant and lazy about it. We are to wait upon the Lord. We are to fast and pray. We are to read and study the Word of God. We are to listen attentively to the Holy Spirit. We are to speak victory, not defeat. We are to lift up His name, not the difficulties and problems. God works when we cooperate with Him.

Dealing with Doubt

Have you ever spoken a positive word of faith and yet had doubt in your heart? Most of us have! You see, it's important that we get the doubt out and feed on faith food. We must get our mouth and heart together, and we can because the Spirit of God lives within us. He can energize us and activate faith for us if we choose to believe. He can impart the gift of faith to us.

It's Up to You and Me!

He has given us the gift of faith for one purpose: to strengthen the Body of Christ. Let's not allow this gift to be dormant. Let's stir ourselves up. Let's stand against depression, sickness, financial decline, and family strife. Let's say we are the delivered, the healed, the blessed, the happy because that is God's will for us. Let's agree with Him and we'll be super victorious.

Chapter 12

Rapha

As Pentecostals we believe in healing from heaven. We believe that Jesus came to save, heal, and deliver. We believe this for a number of reasons not the lease of which is that our God is a Healing God. It is His character to heal.

Healing in His Name

Healing is the very nature of God and this fact is expressed in one of His names: *Jehovah Rapha*. *Jehovah* is His covenant name and *Rapha* means *one who cures, heals, mends, and restores to health.* So He is *The God Who Heals.*

*Exodus 15:26 "If you diligently heed the voice of the Lord your God and do what is right in His sight, give ear to His commandments and keep all His statutes, I will put none of the diseases on you which I brought on the Egyptians. For **I am the Lord who heals you.**"*

Healing in the Atonement

In Pentecost, we believe divine healing is as much a part of the Word of God as salvation is. The atoning Blood of Jesus Christ, shed on the Cross for us, provides benefits for the whole person. That is why we say that *healing is in the Atonement.* When Jesus died on the Cross for our sins, he also took the stripes on His back providing healing for our bodies.

Healing in the Gifts of the Spirit

We also believe in healing because it is listed by Paul as one of the nine gifts of the Spirit.

*1 Cor. 12:8-9 For to one is given . . . to another faith by the same Spirit, to another **gifts of healings** by the same Spirit. . . .*

As is the case with all the gifts, the healing gifts are supernatural. They are not natural, human abilities. We can't **use** these gifts; instead, the Holy Spirit manifests them **as <u>He</u> wills** in response to faith.

In ourselves, we don't have the power to heal anyone. All we can do is cast out sickness in the name of the Lord Jesus. I can't heal you. Benny Hinn can't heal you. Oral Roberts can't heal you. Only Jesus can heal you. He is the One Who has provided healing through the Cross.

The fact that *gifts of healings* is plural suggests there are many sicknesses and diseases. Jesus didn't come to heal only one disease. He came to heal us of *every* sickness and *every* disease. Isn't it wonderful to know that we do not have to tolerate sickness? Jesus didn't come to make us sick. He came to make us well!

Healing in the Prayer of Faith

As Pentecostals, we believe in healing because we read what the Apostle James says about healing and the prayer of faith.

James 5:13-15 Is anyone among you suffering? Let him pray. Is anyone cheerful? Let him sing psalms. Is anyone among you sick? Let him call for the elders of the church, and let them pray for him, anointing him with oil in the name of the Lord. And the prayer of faith will save the sick, and the Lord will raise him up. And if he has committed sins, he will be forgiven. Confess your trespasses to one another, and pray for one another, that you may be healed. The effective, fervent prayer of a righteous man avails much.

The prayer of faith refers to *the gift of faith.* We

normally think of *save* as referring to spiritual salvation, but in this verse *save* means *restore physical health*. Not all sickness comes from sin, but this verse indicates that if sin is the cause of the sickness, it will be forgiven.

Who are *the elders*? The elders are spiritual believers who are mature in the Lord. They are people who have both a special anointing and a deep love for God. They have the power flowing in their lives to pray effectually for the sick. They are a special breed!

Anointing with oil in the name of the Lord doesn't refer to a medical act or a magical incantation. There is no healing in that bottle of olive oil, or whatever kind of oil it is. It's simply a symbol of the Holy Spirit, and it's the Holy Spirit Who brings the healing, not the oil. We can anoint people with oil all we want to, but if the Holy Spirit is not alive in that contact, it won't do anybody any good. It's the symbolic consecration of the sick person together with the joyous blessing and presence of the Holy Spirit that releases God's healing power.

Healing in Jesus' Ministry

We believe in healing because healing was so much a part of Jesus' earthly ministry. By way of example, let's consider the healing of the paralytic in Mark 2.

Mark 2:5, 11 When Jesus saw their faith, he said to the paralytic, "Son, your sins are forgiven you. . . . I say to you, arise, take up your bed, and go your way to your house."

This healing aroused opposition among the religious people because in bringing health to this man, Jesus forgave sin. By doing this, Jesus indicates that, in some cases, there is a connection between sin and sickness.

Mark 2:8-10 [Jesus said,] "Why do you reason about these things in your hearts? Which is easier, to say to the paralytic, 'Your sins are forgiven you,' or to say, 'Arise, take up your bed and walk'? "But that you may know that the Son of Man has power on earth to forgive sins."

The same power to heal the sick was present in the ministries of the twelve that Jesus sent out two-by-two.

Mk. 6:12-13 So they went out and preached that people should repent. And they cast out many demons, and anointed with oil many who were sick and healed them.

Healing in the Book of Acts

As Pentecostals, we believe in healing because we see healing occurring in the Book of Acts after the coming of the Holy Spirit on the Day of Pentecost. Acts 3, for example, records the story of the healing of the lame beggar at the Gate Beautiful. In this case, the power of Jesus' Name brought healing. The name *Jesus* means *Anointed Savior*.

> *Acts 3:6 Then Peter said, "Silver and gold I do not have, but what I do have I give you: In the name of Jesus Christ of Nazareth, rise up and walk.".*

In Acts 28, we read of healing occurring in the ministry of Paul.

> *Acts 28:8-9 And it happened that the father of Publius lay sick of a fever and dysentery. Paul went in to him and prayed, and he laid hands on him and healed him. So when this was done, the rest of those on the island who had diseases also came and were healed.*

Healing Today

The question is often asked: Is diving healing for today?" YES. And I say that with capital letters: YES! Divine healing is for today. Jesus included it in the Great Commission recorded in Mark 16.

Mark 16:15-18 And He [Jesus] said to them, "Go into all the world and preach the gospel to every creature. He who believes and is baptized will be saved; but he who does not believe will be condemned. And these signs will follow those who believe: In My name they will cast out demons; they will speak with new tongues; they will take up serpents; and if they drink anything deadly, it will by no means hurt them; **they will lay hands on the sick, and they will recover.**

This passage says that those who believe will lay hands on the sick and *they __will__ recover*. The supernatural healing of the sick is meant to be a permanent ministry within the church right along with the ministry of evangelizing the world. They are inseparable.

Rom. 11:29 For the gifts and the calling of God are irrevocable.

Our Part in Healing

God heals through the prayer, faith, natural power, and medicine, but Divine healing is the greatest, and we can live in that flow.

Prayer. God's healing power is available to us through the Spirit. The only way we can operate in this power is through prayer. In prayer we learn to hear God's voice and receive His power.

Holiness. We have to live and move in communion with God if we expect to be able to lay hands on the sick and see them healed and delivered. That means we must live a holy life.

Faith. We hold the keys to whether or not we receive healing. God has already provided it, but it's up to us to appropriate it in our lives. Sometimes it seems we would rather just suffer and endure. "How are you feeling today?" "Oh, my back is hurting so bad!" "Oh, the Devil has got me!" "I've got the flu again." Come on, now! Why praise the name of Satan?

The Holy Spirit. The same power that was available to Jesus and the Apostles is available in the church today through the same Holy Spirit. Healing is one way that the power of the Holy Spirit is released.

Chapter 13

Power
Beyond
the Ordinary

Our God is a Miracle-Working God. When we've done all we can do and it's still not enough, we need the intervention of the mighty, supernatural power of God. We need a miracle!

The Gift of the Working of Miracles

1 Cor. 12:10a to another [is given] the working of miracles

The gift of working of miracles is a power gift. It is a manifestation of power beyond the ordinary course of natural law. It is the divine empowerment to do something that could not occur naturally.

What Is *A Miracle?*

In one sense, to God there is no such thing as a miracle. A miracle is a miracle only from a human point of view. From our perspective, everything that God does is a miracle.

Do you know that you are one of God's miracles? You know your life, and you know how God has preserved you. You know that He has rescued you from a life of sin, and you know He has healed you from sickness. You know He has delivered you and will yet deliver you from the snares of the Devil as you trust in Him. You are a miracle!

You Can Be a Miracle Worker!

Have you ever thought of yourself as a miracle worker? We are in the sense that God needs us to bring forth miracles.

1 Cor. 12:29 Are all apostles? Are all prophets? Are all teachers? Are all workers of miracles?

The answer to all of these questions, of course, is *no*. But, on the other hand, we all can be workers of miracles because all we need is the power of the Holy Ghost working in our lives. In our own strength, we can never perform miracles. It is the power of God flowing through our lives that produces miracles.

The working of miracles is a supernatural event. It is the intervention of God in the natural realm. It is the Spirit of God countering and defeating the forces of evil.

The working of miracles is closely akin to the other power gifts: gifts of faith and healings. A miracle comes through faith and faith in God produces miracles. We can't work up a miracle. It comes as the Spirit wills, normally in response to faith.

As believers, we have the power of God coursing through our beings. Let's rise to the occasion. Let's wake up, Church! Let's quit being a stubborn, frozen people and let's become the dynamic force in the world we are to meant to be!

Energized and Dynamic

1 Cor. 12:10 To another working of miracles?

The Greek words that we translate *working of miracles* are *energemata dunameon*. These can also be translated *operations of powers*.

The derivations of the words are very interesting. *Energemata* is the Greek word from which we get the English word *energy*. *Dunameon* is the Greek word from which we get the English word *dynamite*. Imagine! The energized operations of the dynamite of God!

Acts 1:8 says we receive *dunamis* [dynamite] *when the Holy Spirit comes upon us.* We are powerful people when the Spirit comes upon us! We aren't wimps! We are full of the energized dynamite of God!

This gift of energy or dynamite is God doing something of an explosive nature.

Jesus tells us,

Lk. 10:19 "Behold, I give you the authority to trample on serpents and scorpions, and over all the power [dunamin] of the enemy, and nothing shall by any means hurt you."

Sometimes we can't comprehend the fact that we have this kind of power. But we do! We have the power to stop everything the Devil throws at us.

We really have to examine ourselves in the light all of this. Can we honestly say that we are exhibiting this energy and dynamism? Are we experiencing the explosiveness of God? Or are we dead? We stand up to sing. We sit down to listen to people talk. We just go through the motions. Let's get the dynamite ignited!

Does anybody really want to be part of something that is dead, indifferent, cold? No. We all want to be part of something that is energized and dynamic. The church has the greatest opportunity to be the most energized and dynamic people in the whole world!

God Made a Donkey Talk!

One of the great examples of the working of a miracle is found in Numbers 22:22-40 where God spoke through Balaam's donkey! God didn't speak in this manner for the novelty of it. It was a serious effort to get Balaam's attention. Balaam was out of God's will when, unbeknown to Balaam, an angel appeared repeatedly to his donkey in order to hinder his advance toward destruction. Balaam couldn't understand his donkey's unusual behavior and finally, in anger, he struck the donkey three time. At this point, God caused the donkey to speak.

Numbers 22:28   Then the Lord opened the mouth of the donkey, and she said to Balaam, "What have I done to you, that you have struck me these three times?"

The result was that Balaam repented of his sin and again became useful to the Lord. In the same way in dealing with us, if God has to, He will release a miracle to get our attention.

Delivered from Lions

Daniel 6:10-23 tells how God delivered Daniel from the lions' den where he had been thrown as punishment for worshipping God. God delivered Daniel by closing the lions' mouths. This Old Testament story illustrates the working of miracles and faith.

> *Daniel 6:16-22 [The king said to Daniel,] "Your God, whom you serve continually, he will deliver you." . . . "Daniel, servant of the living God, has your God, whom you serve continually been able to deliver you from the lions?" Then Daniel said to the king, "O king, live forever! My God sent His angel and shut the lions' mouths, so that they have not hurt me, because I was found innocent before Him; and also, O king, I have done no wrong before you."*

Daniel was taken out of the den unharmed. He had faith in God and God had worked a miracle on his behalf.

Samson's Supernatural Strength

Another example of the working of miracles is found in the life of Samson.

Judges 14:5 So Samson went down to Timnah with his father and mother, and came to the vineyards of Timnah. Now to his surprise, a young lion came roaring against him. And the Spirit of the Lord came mightily upon him, and he tore the lion apart as one would have torn apart a young goat, though he had nothing in his hand.

Here the Spirit of the Lord empowered Samson to perform an extraordinary deed. He enabled Samson to tear apart the lion with his bare hands! What was the key to all of this? Verse 6 tells us: *The Spirit of the Lord came mightily upon him.*

On three other occasions in the story, Samson enjoyed supernatural strength. In each situation, this mighty, supernatural strength came upon him when the Spirit of the Lord came upon him.

Think about it! Samson did mighty deeds when the Spirit of the Lord came upon him. He was not capable of these deeds apart from divine intervention. It was the Holy Spirit enablement that made the difference.

I see a similarity in the church today. There's something missing! What is it? It's the Spirit of the Lord! Where is the Pentecostal power we once experienced? I'm afraid we buried it in the Charismatic Movement! What I mean is this: the Charismatic Movement taught us that we could do anything we wanted to do in our own strength. That's what they taught. I know because I sat in those teaching sessions! I know what they taught. They told us we could speak in tongues by listening to someone who did and mimic them. They taught us to have faith in faith instead of faith in God. That's not how it is, Friend! We need the Holy Spirit.

Jesus and Miracles

Jesus depended on the Holy Spirit to do what was impossible in His humanity. Do you remember, for example, how, at the wedding feast in Canaan of Galilee He turned water to wine? It was the first miracle he performed (Jn. 1:11), and the disciples believed on Him because of it.

On another occasion, He fed five thousand men plus women and children with five loaves and two fish (Mt. 14:13-21). He took the one lunch and thanked God for it. Then He broke it and passed it around to the hungry people. That bread and those fish kept multiplying until everyone had enough to eat. Not only that, but there were twelve baskets full left over!

Paul and Miracles

Miracles didn't stop when Jesus went away. He sent the Holy Spirit to be with us always and so the Source of Miracles is with us. Paul experienced this on many occasions.

In Lystra, the power of the Spirit healed a crippled man as faith came to him through Paul's preaching (Acts 14:8).

One night Paul was still preaching at midnight when a young man named Eutychus fell asleep and tumbled from the window sill where he had been sitting. The fall killed him (Acts 20:7-12). But that wasn't the end of the story!

Acts 20:10-12 But Paul went down, fell on him, and embracing him said, "Do not trouble yourselves, for his life is in him." Now when he had come up, had broken bread and eaten, and talked a long while, even till daybreak, he departed. And they brought the young man in alive, and they were not a little comforted.

In other words, great joy went through the

crowd because this young man who was dead was now alive! Miracles will bring joy to a church!

Miracles Now!

The working of miracles didn't stop in the Bible. They are still occurring today. The lame are being healed. The deaf are hearing. The blind are seeing. The storms are being stilled. Financial provision is being released. Why? It's because the Holy Spirit is with us. It's because people of faith are looking to the Lord. It's because Our God is a Mighty God and He cares about you and me!

> *Acts 2:38 Then Peter said to them, "Repent, and let every one of you be baptized in the name of Jesus Christ for the remission of sins; and you shall receive the gift of the Holy Spirit. For the promise is to you and to your children, and to all who are afar off, as many as the Lord our God will call."*

I rest my case! The working of miracles is for the church today. Are you ready? Are you ready to receive your miracle? Are you ready to be used by God? Are you ready?

Chapter 14

Supernatural Information

Many times over the years I have stopped to thank God for the privilege of growing up in a Pentecostal home and a Pentecostal church. I am thankful for the tremendous opportunities I've had to learn the ways of the Lord. As a child, I would sit for three and four hours at a time in meeting after meeting in that second pew between Mother and Dad. I would see the mighty demonstrations of the power of God. I long for a return of that mighty outpouring of the Holy Spirit in our churches. As we continue this study, may we be stirred to welcome the Spirit with the fervency and devotion that those dear people did.

The Revelation Gifts

Three gifts of the Spirit have been called the

revelation gifts. They are the word of knowledge, the word of wisdom, and discerning of spirits. These gifts supernaturally reveal information that would otherwise not be available in those circumstances at that time.

The gift of the word of knowledge may be called the word of *God's* knowledge. Out of His limitless storehouse of knowledge, He supernaturally imparts fragments of information for a specific purpose to a person who has no other means of accessing that information. This information reveals facts that have occurred in the past or that are taking place in the present.

God always has a reason for releasing this holy, precious gift. It contributes to godly living by revealing His will concerning a person, a situation, or an event. Normally the gift has to do with meeting a pressing need that cannot wait for the normal course of events to unfold.

Some people have misused this gift. Some have tried to counterfeit it. They seem to want to appear more spiritual than others. They also tend to be interested excessively in other people's business. These attitudes are not pleasing to God! Furthermore, people who have these attitudes easily fall prey to demonic, familiar spirits and psychic phenomena. This gift is not a toy!

Words of Knowledge in the Old Testament

1 Kings 19:14

Have you ever felt that you were the only one faithfully serving God? Elijah the Prophet felt that way.

1 Kings 19:14 "I have been very zealous for the Lord God of Hosts; because the children of Israel have forsaken Your covenant, torn down your altars, and killed your prophets with the sword. I alone am left, and they seek to take my life."

God wasn't pleased with Elijah's attitude. He used the word of knowledge to confront him about it. He revealed something to Elijah that only He knew.

1 Kings 19:18 Yet I have reserved seven thousand in Israel, all whose knees have not bowed to Baal, and every mouth that has not kissed him."

This word of knowledge pulled Elijah up short! He wilted! Suddenly he knew that he had been consumed with self-centeredness. He knew that he had turned from God to a self-righteous attitude. He was having a real pity party! And it was time to repent!

Our attitude, like that of Elijah's, can easily slip into self-centeredness. "Oh poor me! I'm the only one left to carry out the work!" I'm the only one good enough!" That self-righteousness gets hold of us sometimes, doesn't it? But we're wrong and we need to repent!

2 Kings 5:20-27

Naaman was a wealthy Syrian general who had come to Elisha and had received a remarkable healing. After being healed, Naaman turned to Elisha and said, "Elisha, I don't want your offering. Take your healing and go home!"

But Gehazi, Elisha's servant, was secretly at work on his own behalf. He pursued Namaan and accepted the gifts for himself. Meanwhile God was revealing Gehazi's secret sin to Elisha by a word of knowledge (v. 26). When Elisha confronted him about it, he lied. Immediately he was stricken with leprosy.

Like Gehazi, we too might be tempted to take possession of something the wrong way and then thank God for it! It's possible too that we might commit a second sin to cover the first.

2 Kings 6:8-12

During a time of war between Syria and Israel, the king of Syria was astounded that the king of Israel always knew where he was encamped. He assumed there was a traitor in his midst, but one of his servants said, "No, that's not it!" He told the king, "Elisha, the prophet who is in Israel, tells the king of Israel the words that you speak in your bedroom" (2 Kings 6:12). God was giving Elisha words of knowledge.

1 Sam. 10:17-27

This passage tells the story of the coronation of Saul as King of Israel. Saul was a shy and modest person and when they were looking for him to crown him, he was hiding. Some translations say he was hiding *behind a stump* (KJV); others, *behind the equipment* (NJK); and others, *behind the baggage.* The point is, he was hiding! When it became obvious that he was the one God had chosen to be king, it was only through a word of knowledge that he could be found.

There is a principle here that applies today: God knows everything. He always knows where we are, and he always knows where everything is. My mother looks to the Lord this way. If we happen to be looking for something, she'll ask, "Holy Spirit, show me where it is." Inevitably she will find it in a matter seconds!

Words of Knowledge in the New Testament

Examples of the word of knowledge occur in the New Testament. Jesus, Peter, and Paul all experienced this gift of the Spirit.

John 4:1-26

When the Samaritan woman arrived at Jacob's Well at noon to draw water, Jesus was already there alone. It was unusual for a Jew to talk to a woman in public, and it was likewise unusual for a Jew to speak to a Samaritan. When Jesus asked the woman for a drink of water, she was amazed, but He went on to tell her that if she had made the same request of Him, He would have given her living water and she would never thirst again!

Continuing His conversation with the woman, Jesus described in accurate detail the condition of her life. She had been passed from one man to another five times, as was the custom when a woman did not bear a male child, and she was now in the charge of a sixth man who had not taken her in marriage. That Jesus knew this astounded her, and His knowledge and concern captured her attention. He did something for this woman that He seldom did, and that is He clearly identified Himself as the

Messiah. He said to her, "I who speak to you am He [the Messiah]" (Jn. 4:26). As a result, this poor village woman became an evangelist proclaiming Jesus! John tells us,

> *Jn. 4:28-30 The woman then left her waterpot, went her way into the city, and said to the men, "Come, see a man who told me all things that I ever did. Could this be the Christ?"*

Acts 10:19-20

Peter was fasting and praying one day when he had a dramatic experience of the word of knowledge.

> *Acts 10:19-20 While Peter thought about the vision, the Spirit of the Lord said to him, "Three men are seeking you. Arise therefore, go down and be with them, doubting nothing; for I have sent them."*

These men had been sent by Cornelius, a God-fearing Gentile who lived in Caesarea. Cornelius had been praying when a holy angel instructed him to send for Peter (v. 22), whom the angel said, would tell him the words of truth. When Cornelius' messengers arrived where Peter was staying, he was ready. God had worked on both ends by words of knowledge.

Today God always works on both ends. He never does anything half-way. He does a complete work. That is the kind of God we serve!

1 Corinthians 12:7-11

Paul gives clear instructions to the Corinthian church concerning the operation of the word of knowledge as well as the other gifts. The Corinthian believers had been very familiar with demonic and psychic phenomena before they got saved. It was especially important, then, that they understand how to relate to the pure word of knowledge and the other gifts of the Spirit.

These manifestations of God's power are missing from so many Pentecostal churches today. This seems to be the case for two main reasons. First many Pentecostal churches have become seduced by evil and worldly spirits. Secondly, many Pentecostal people today have never understood the gifts of the Spirit and have never been taught about them. In a sense, we were thrown the gifts, and we were told to take them and use them, but we were never taught how. We tried to operate in them, but more often than not, we fell flat on our faces!

The Word of Knowledge Today

Friend, the gifts of the Spirit are to operate in our lives. When they do, we'll see souls saved. We'll see the captives set free. We'll see the sick healed. People once again will fear God.

Work Provided.

In one of my revival meetings in Torrance, California, a woman came to me for prayer. Her husband had lost his job and they had no money. She didn't know what she was going to do! Her husband's former employer told him he wouldn't be called back for several months. As I prayed with her, God spoke to me, "There is a call coming through for him to go to work." When she came back to the meeting the next night she was so excited! God had already fulfilled His word. The woman's husband had already been called back to work.

Financial Worries Quelled.

On another occasion when I was holding meetings in Torrance, a woman came to me and said, "Preacher, I have so many bills that have to be paid tomorrow and I don't have the money to pay them. Please pray for me."

As I prayed for her, God began to reveal to

me what was happening in her life. He said, "Tell her that there is a check on the way and it will be in her mailbox tomorrow." When she came back to church the next night, she could hardly wait to stand up and tell the people what God had done. She said, "The check was big enough to pay all of my bills."

That's the kind of God we serve. When we need an answer, we can go to Him. He will show us what we need to know. God cares.

How to Operate in the Gift of the Word of Knowledge

Personal Holiness

We need all the gifts of the Spirit operating in our lives, but they will operate only in a holy life, for the Spirit is holy and cannot operate in a defiled vessel. That may be Old-Time Pentecostal teaching, but it's also the Word of God! We can operate in the gifts of God's Holy Spirit only when we are living a holy, sanctified life before Him. Years ago, when these gifts worked in great power in the church, people lived their whole lives before God.

Dependence on God

In those bygone days, the Pentecostal believers may not have had much education, but they knew how to depend on the Lord. They were educated in holy living. Perhaps with less academic education, we may have continued to depend more fully on God. We're not against education, but in many cases, we have allowed education to take the place of the power of God. We think we can work things out in our own little minds! We think we don't need the Holy Spirit anymore to teach us. How wrong we are! As a result, we don't have the power we once had! We don't have the working of the word of knowledge that we once had. We are depending on our own knowledge instead. let's turn it around!

Fear of God

In those days, the Pentecostal believers not only depended on God, but they also feared God. They had a healthy fear of God's awesome power. They understood true reverence for God. We don't fear God that way any more. We've been lulled to sleep by the idea that God is a loving God. Yes, He is a loving God, but that's not all He is! He is also a Holy God. He says, "If you fail to serve me, I will throw you into the lake of fire where the worm never dies." There will be burning, wailing, and gnashing of teeth. People seem totally unaware of this! They don't fear God as they should.

Respect for the Pentecostal Experience

They recognized and respected the Pentecostal experience and the gifts of the Holy Ghost. They sought God with all their hearts and allowed Him to cleanse them and empower them.

Those who were living in sin wouldn't come to church back in those early days. They were afraid of the Holy presence of God. I think it's fair to say that today that's not the case! In fact, the opposite is true! Today they don't come because nothing is happening!

It's time for us to seek the Lord until we know what He is saying to the church today. It's time for us to know what He is saying to us as individuals. It's time for the word of knowledge to be released in our midst so that we can be overcomers in life. If we come to church with a frown, we should leave with a smile. If we come to church hurting, we should leave in victory.

Where is the body of Christ? Are we ready to be filled once again with the Spirit of Christ? It's time for cleansing and a fresh filling. It's time for a fresh baptism of the Holy Ghost and fire.

Chapter 15

Who Needs
Crystal Ball Gazers?

We all need wisdom! *Wisdom* is the skill, intelligence, discretion, thoughtfulness, and prudence that helps us prosper in everything we do. There is natural wisdom that we gain in everyday life and there is supernatural wisdom that Paul calls *the word of wisdom*. It is the second of the revelation gifts of the Spirit listed in 1 Corinthians 12:8.

The gift of *the word of wisdom* does not refer to natural, human wisdom that gives us success in everyday life. This kind of wisdom is found in what is called the Wisdom Literature of the Old Testament. The Wisdom Literature includes Job, Proverbs, Ecclesiastes, and Song of Solomon.

My wife and I like to draw wisdom from these books. Sometimes as I drive her to work, she reads a few Proverbs and we discuss them. This is so helpful in giving the wisdom she needs to deal with all the different circumstances that pop up in the run of a day on the job.

The gift of the word of wisdom is different from this. It is a revelation gift of the Spirit. A *word of wisdom* is *a message or utterance characterized by wisdom that comes through the inspiration of the Holy Spirit.*

In the word of wisdom, God reveals information supernaturally to us. It is information that comes from outside the bounds of our natural processes. It is something we do not and cannot know in the natural. It is information the mind cannot perceive. It doesn't come by what we hear and or see. There is nothing natural about the word of wisdom. It is spiritual.

The word of wisdom is not just a gift of wisdom. It is a gift of **a word** of wisdom. It is a fragment from the total wisdom of God. It is a portion of His unlimited all-knowing. God sees it all! He knows our lives down to the smallest detail. He knows all about everything that is happening all the time. Because He knows things about the future that we do not know, He prepares us so that we are able to take care of whatever comes.

This may sound like prophecy, but it's important to distinguish between the simple inspiration gift of prophecy and the word of wisdom.

Whereas the word of wisdom involves the element of revelation, the gift of prophecy does not. This is born out by Paul in 1 Corinthians.

1 Cor. 14:3 But he who prophecies speaks edification and exhortation and comfort to men.

When the Spirit moves us to speak out in the congregation foretelling the future, we have left the gift of prophecy and have entered into the gift of the word of wisdom. The word of wisdom is the gift whereby we foresee the future.

When God gives a word of His wisdom, He is revealing something that has not yet come to pass. Every prophet in the Bible operated in the word of wisdom as does every prophet today.

Revealing the Hidden Things

The word of wisdom unveils in part the purpose of God on earth. Let's see how the Apostle Paul explained it to the Corinthians.

1 Cor. 2:7 But we speak the wisdom of God in a mystery, the hidden wisdom which God ordained before the ages of our glory.

When we think of a *mystery*, we think of something that is difficult to understand. That is not what the word *mystery* means in the New Testament, however. In this verse, it refers to *the truth hidden in God's mind until He chooses to disclose it.*

God reveals truth according to His plan and schedule, not according to ours. The word of wisdom, then, reveals aspects of mystery. It involves speaking portions of hidden things known to God. His wisdom far exceeds all earthly wisdom. It is beyond our range or ability. That is, in fact, why we call it *a mystery.*

The primary mystery is God's plan of redemption devised even before the earth came into being. It is a mystery from our human vantage point, but it is not a mystery from God's point of view. We have been let in on the meaning of this mystery through the coming of the Lord Jesus Christ. In fact, had He not come, the plan of redemption would have remained a complete mystery. But the hidden knowledge of God's plan to redeem humanity, was revealed through Him.

How the Gift Comes

Again, let me say that the word of wisdom has no relationship to natural knowledge. We must understand this. A person with very little education can operate in the gift of the word of wisdom. It doesn't take a college degree! What it does take is a relationship with Jesus Christ through the Holy Spirit. It's on our knees that we build a relationship with God that makes us available for God to use. So we receive words of wisdom on our knees, not through earning a college degree!

Another thing to remember about receiving words of wisdom is that when the Holy Spirit moves through us, it's not us and God. It's God in us doing it. We must get *I* out of the way. We must allow God to be the center of our lives and churches. It is then, and only then, that He will move through us supernaturally.

The Power of the Gift

The gift of the word of wisdom has the power to transform the world. In fact, if the gifts of the Spirit were to operate in the church, the world would stand in awe and total fascination!

But what do we find today? Instead of the gifts operating as they should, people are allowing the operation of demonic spirits and psychic phenomena. Counterfeit demonstrations of the gifts of the Holy Spirit have people mesmerized!

The mind is the battlefield. The Devil is unrelenting in his efforts to confuse and distract us from Truth. Even in lighthearted entertainment we are being seeded with magic and witchcraft. In fact, in our day, a wave of the occult is sweeping the world. Fortune telling is rampant. Crystal ball gazing and playing with ouiga boards are popular pastimes. Tea leaf reading and palm reading are accepted with no understanding of their devastating spiritual implications. The Devil has so many schemes to capture the minds and hearts of people who hunger to know the future!

One of the greatest methods used to enslave people is the horoscope column in the daily newspaper. Some people are so bound they won't leave the house unless the horoscope tells them they can. It's amazing how many Christians are bewitched by these horoscopes. If we were wrapped up in the Holy Spirit, we wouldn't even consider the possibility of consulting the horoscopes. We would face each new day with peace and anticipation, looking to the Holy Spirit to guide, protect, empower, and prosper our way. Godly confidence, not fear, would infuse every aspect of our lives.

We ought not to be manipulated and misled by the Devil and his cohorts! The Holy Spirit has given us Himself and His gifts to combat every attack of the enemy. Our part is to cultivate an intimate relationship with the Lord, and His part is to empower us according to His will in dealing with each and every need. He is faithful to do His part. Let us be faithful to do our part.

A Better Way

1 Cor. 12:31 But earnestly desire the best gifts and yet I show you a more excellent way.

Friend, when we truly desire the gifts we will find that they are readily available to us. They are not just written about in the Bible. They are in the Bible so that we can know about them and desire them earnestly. When we do, what a wonderful, powerful, dynamic relationship will emerge with God! The more excellent way of love (1 Cor. 13) will indeed come to life in us through the gifts of the Holy Spirit.

The Word of Wisdom in the Old Testament

Old Testament characters experienced the word of wisdom.

- God gave **Noah** a word of wisdom concerning the flood (Gen. 6:12-22). It had not even rained at that point in history! But God gave him instructions to build an ark, to do something that seemed totally bizarre! From that day for the next one hundred and twenty years, Noah waited expectantly knowing that God would destroy the earth.

- **Daniel** too received words of wisdom by the Spirit. His came in the form of great visions. He saw empires rise and fall on the stage of human history. He even identified the characteristics of each empire.

- **Ezekiel** received words of wisdom. In Ezekiel 38 and 39, he dramatically foretold the whole future. He said that armies from the north would come against countries of unwalled villages (38:1-11). In Ezekiel's day all the villages had walls to fend off predators and enemies, but today the villages of Israel have no walls. God told Ezekiel what would happen. He said "from the north" they would come, and this was before Russia was even in existence. Today, Russia is friendly, but one day, what was predicted in prophecy will come to pass.

- **David** revealed by a word of wisdom recorded in Psalm 22:6-18 how the Messiah would come and how He would die.

- **Joel**, by divine inspiration, revealed how, in the last days, the Holy Spirit would be poured out upon all flesh (Joel 2:28-30).
- **Isaiah** 53:1-12 may be the greatest prophecy of the Bible because it describes the nature of the Messiah. He describes the kind of person He would be, how He would die, and what that would mean to us. By His stripes, for example, we would be healed. In Isaiah's day, stripes were not even known as a form of punishment!

The Word of Wisdom in the New Testament

The occurrence of the word of wisdom is also reported in the New Testament.

- In the **Gospels**, Jesus foretold the destruction of the temple at Jerusalem. He also foretold the signs that would accompany His return to earth.
- In the **Epistles**, Paul revealed what would come to pass in the last days. Also, according to Acts 23:11, God revealed to Paul that he would preach the Gospel in Rome.

How the Word of Wisdom Comes

The Holy Spirit releases the word of wisdom in many different ways.

- **Joseph** received the word of wisdom through interpreting a dream about the future. God showed him his whole life when he was but seventeen years of age.

- **Daniel** received the word of wisdom in a night vision.

- **Ezekiel** was carried into the Spirit and had a revelation.

- The Apostle **John** was caught up in the Spirit on the Lord's day and God gave him the entire Book of Revelation.

A Word of Caution!

God knows the total past, the total present, and the total future. It's that simple. On the other hand, when we receive the gift of the word of wisdom, we don't know all that God knows.

It's painful to watch some immature folks who receive what they believe to be words of wisdom. They become *know-it-alls*. Don't people like to strut their stuff? "Thus sayeth God. . . ." "God told me this!" And "God told me that!"

But we don't know it all no matter how intimate our relationship is with God.

By the way, God is not going to give His gifts to us if we have a know-it-all attitude. God doesn't exalt us. We are to exalt Him. If we lift ourselves up because a gift or two happens to manifest through us, we are ready for a great fall.

Awake!

We go, go, go seven days a week. We get so wrapped up in working, in fighting the elements of this world, in just making it through another day! That's just what the Devil wants! Many times, we make our own problems and the Devil simply takes advantage of our dilemma. To prevent this, we need to get close to God and be willing to let go of those things in our lifestyle that divert us from serving God 100 percent.

The gifts of revelation are helpful tools in living this overcoming, Spirit-led life that is our responsibility and privilege as believers. They provide an in-depth revelation of God's power and they activate this mighty power on our behalf. With these gifts, we stand in the holy presence of God. It's important then that we stop and listen, that we take to heart what God is saying and doing today.

Friend, this is the day to put our relationship with the Lord first. We need an old-fashioned gully-washer-outpouring of the Holy Ghost. We need this cleansing and empowerment! We need to get the message, Church! God is saying, "Awake, Church! Allow My Spirit to move in your midst."

Everyday I pray,

Oh God, help the church to see what is needed today. Do whatever you have to do to stir our hearts to want the Holy Spirit operating in our lives. Amen.

Chapter 16

No One
Will Ever Know . . .

The gift of discerning of spirits is the third revelation gift listed by Paul in 1 Corinthians 12:10. The gift of discerning of spirits is a supernatural power given by the Holy Spirit. It enables us to detect and identify activity in the spirit realm. It helps us determine the source of what is being said or done.

This gift is not primarily the discerning of the activity of holy spirits or demonic spirits. It gives understanding of the human spirit. It reveals what force is motivating a person to behave in a certain way. It answers the critical question: Is this person's behavior coming from God, the flesh, or the Devil? With spiritual activity so prevalent in our day, we definitely need this gift in operation.

We cannot discern activity in the spirit realm by our natural abilities to feel, hear, see, smell, or taste. Nothing physical or natural can be brought to bear in the gift of discerning of spirits. It is not a metaphysical operation that we initiate by something we do. It comes because the Holy Spirit chooses to open our eyes to the spirit realm.

The Gift of Suspicion?

This gift comes by the will of the Holy Spirit and is not initiated in any way by the power of the natural mind. Of course this is true of all the gifts but it needs to be stressed again when talking about this gift. People often think they are moving in this gift when, in fact, they are not. In other words, people often misinterpret natural insight as discerning of spirits.

The discerning of spirits it is not the gift of suspicion. Sometimes a person's unique personality might lead us to suppose negative or positive things about him or her. In cases like this we have to be careful. We must not confuse the expression of a human spirit with a demonic spirit or with the Holy Spirit.

Some people wrongly claim to have the gift of discernment. They mean well, but really there is no such thing as *the gift of discernment*. It is *the gift of discerning of spirits*. We cannot go around saying, "I discern this thing is not of God." It's the discerning of spirits. It's spirits we discern.

Is It God? The Flesh? Or the Devil?

The gift of discerning of spirits operates in three different areas.

- *The Divine.* The discerning of spirits enables us to detect the activity of the Holy Spirit and God's holy angels. We must know what is of God and what is not of God.

- *The Demonic.* The discerning of spirits also enables us to identify the activity of the Devil and demonic spirits. This is so important because the Devil is a deceiver and comes as an angel of light (2 Cor. 11:14), and his servants come as wolves in sheep's clothing (Mt. 7:15).

- *The Human.* The discerning of spirits enables us to determine when something is coming from the natural, human spirit. As believers, we are to be led by the Holy Spirit and not by the human spirit or flesh.

The Benefits of the Gift

The gift of discerning of spirits is very beneficial to the church.

- It can provide protection against false doctrines and lies.
- The gift of the discerning of spirits can help bring life into a church.
- It can enable churches to choose the right people for ministry positions.

Have you ever wondered why our churches have so many problems? One of the main reasons is that we don't know who is to do what, and often the wrong people get in the wrong positions. Especially in smaller churches, we often have to beg people to take responsibility, and we often end up turning over responsibility to whoever will do the job. Now God has gifted each believer with specific gifts for specific jobs, and it's important that the right people be in the right positions! There are times this happens only by the operation of discerning of spirits. Spiritual things are spiritually discerned.

A Magician's Evil Heart Exposed

The story of Simon the Sorcerer in Acts 8 illustrates the working of the gift of discerning of spirits. Simon had been watching Peter and John as they laid hands on the believers to receive the gift of the Holy Spirit. Simon, who was a magician by trade, thought, "This power is greater than what I possess! If I had the power they have, it would make me a big man! I'll persuade this man to sell me this gift."

So Simon offered to buy this power. He didn't understand that this power was a divinely bestowed gift! *A gift* is something that is not and cannot be bought. Nor can a gift be earned, for anything that is earned cannot be a gift. It is no longer *a gift* if it is bought or earned. *A gift* to be *a gift* must be freely bestowed. Furthermore, a gift is given, not because of the receiver of the gift, but because of the grace of the giver. In the case of the gifts of the Spirit, the gifts are given because of the grace of God. We can never earn or buy them. That is why they are called *grace gifts* or the *charismata*, the Greek word meaning *grace gifts*.

When Simon tried to buy the power demonstrated in the life of Peter and John, he was motivated by an ungodly spirit. He was exhibiting his evil desire to exercise control over other people. He saw this power as a means to gain greater control and personal recognition.

Simon desired a good thing, that is, the power of the Holy Spirit in his life, but he desired it for the wrong reason! The gifts are given for the glory of God and the benefit of others, not for our own gain or gratification. He wanted to be in the limelight. (It is to our shame that many today are in the ministry for the same reason!)

Peter's response was sharp! He said,

"Your money perish with you, because you thought that the gift of God could be purchased with money! You have neither part nor portion in this matter, for your heart is not right in the sight of God" (Acts 8:20-21).

We wonder if Simon was a Christian. We read,

Acts 8:13 Then Simon himself also believed; and when he was baptized he continued with Philip, and was amazed, seeing the miracles and signs which were done.

In verse 21, however, Peter says, *"You have neither part nor portion in this matter, for your heart is not right in the sight of God."* If a person's heart is not right with God, is that person a Christian? Simon had been baptized in water, but his heart was not right with God. That seems to be the determining factor.

Peter commanded,

Acts 8:22-23 "Repent therefore of this your wickedness, and pray God if perhaps the thought of your heart may be forgiven you. For I see that you are poisoned by bitterness and bound by iniquity"

The working of the gift of discerning of spirits is very clear in this story. Peter saw what was happening in the spirit world. He was able to discern the spirit that motivated Simon.

Blessing: A Benefit or A Motive?

One of the greatest failures of many believers today is that they try to buy God's blessing. They give their tithes and offerings with that in mind. This is not how blessing comes. Blessing must be the benefit <u>not</u> the motive!

I think of my Dad who was as faithful a giver as anyone could ever be. He was on disability for years due to severe arthritis. As soon as he received his disability check each month, he would give his ten percent and other offerings. Eventually Dad was healed. I believe it was, in part, due to his obedience in giving. He didn't give to get. He received the benefit in the area of his need. He needed healing and that's what he received.

Magician Exposed

Acts 13:4-12 gives another example of the discerning of spirits in operation. Paul and Silas were on the island of Cyprus when they encountered Elymas the Sorcerer who tried to hinder their ministry efforts. Through the operation of the gift of discerning of spirits, his effort were exposed and the proconsul was saved.

Paul's words were straight to the point:

Acts 13: 9-11 Paul, filled with the Holy Spirit, looked intently at him [Elymas] and said, "Oh full of all deceit and all fraud, you son of the devil, you enemy of all righteousness, will you not cease perverting the straight ways of the Lord? And now, indeed, the hand of the Lord is upon you, and you shall be blind, not seeing the sun for a time." And immediately a dark mist fell on him, and he went around seeking someone to lead him by the hand.

Imagine walking up to someone and saying, "You son of the Devil!" You might not live! Paul certainly had to be in the Spirit to say that!

Paul discerned this man's evil intent. This is not something that happens in the natural. People like Elymus look just as natural and normal as anybody else. Outward appearance normally doesn't tell us that a person is a fortune teller, a palm reader, or a witch. They look like you and me. They may even work beside us on the job. If we cannot discern the spirits, we're in trouble.

Church People Exposed

Acts 5:1-11 tells another powerful story of the working of the gift of discerning of spirits. In this story, Barnabas sold all of his property and gave the proceeds to the church. Ananias and Sapphira also sold their property, but when they got the money they decided it was too much to give to the church. They withheld a portion of it but pretended that they had given it all. They thought no one would ever know! They ignored the word of caution in Numbers 32:23.

Numbers 32:23 But if you do not do so, then take note. You have sinned against the Lord and be sure your sin will find you out.

This verse is not talking about sin being un-covered. It declares that an evil deed will come back on the evil doer. It expresses the truth: What we sow is what we will reap.

When Ananias presented to Peter his bag of gold and silver, he said, "We are going to give all the money to the church." He lied and immedi-ately the gift of discerning of spirits alerted Peter, who then asked, "All of it?" "Yes," said Ananias, "all of it." Peter was willing to give him the benefit of the doubt, so he asked him again. When he continued to lie, he fell dead instantly!

Three hours later, Sapphira his wife walked in proudly. She said, "We sold our property and gave all the money to the church." Peter asked, "Sapphira, was all the money in the bag when Ananias left the house?" And she replied, "Oh, yes." And she too fell dead.

Friend, you don't lie to the Holy Spirit!

Cleaning Up God's House

I remember these gifts operating in the church when I was a child. Some people were afraid to come to church because they knew their sin would be exposed by the Holy Spirit.

The church today could certainly use a good housecleaning. If the gift of discerning of spirits were operating, imagine what would happen!

Are we willing to be cleansed? Are we willing to be clean vessels that the Holy Spirit can use whenever and however He might choose?

We need to be available to the Holy Spirit to operate in discerning of spirits. It is a crucial gift that enables us to appraise motives. It gives us the ability to see into the realm of the spirit and to see what is behind the problems that beset our churches. God has a purpose in this gift, and that purpose is to keep the church pure and holy.

Conclusion

My life with the Lord began when I was very young. I was about four years old when Mother and Dad came into Pentecost. It's all I've ever known. I can't imagine Christianity without the Pentecostal experience.

My first recollection of a serious encounter with the Lord happened when I was six years old. In a country church in Pennsylvania, I knelt alone at the back of the church. There I cried out to Jesus to save my soul.

A year later, another encounter with the Lord changed my life forever. I was attending an old-fashioned tent meeting with Mom. I can still remember the old tent with its wooden benches, saw-dust floor, and puddles of water left over from the afternoon thunder shower.

On this particular evening, I was in my usual place beside my Mom worshipping God. Those were the days when meetings lasted at least two or three hours or more every evening. This particular night, as the altar service went on and on, I grew restless and hungry. Like most little boys, I asked my Mom for a quarter to go to the snack bar. I bought a bag of chips, a candy bar, and a pop--and I still had a nickel left over! When I finished, I went back for another quarter and bought more chips, candy, and pop. I was still hungry when we began the drive home that night!

As we drove along the country road, I sang songs of praise to the Lord with Mom and our friends. I had no idea that that something special was about to happen to me! Sitting in the front seat, I began to feel something I had never felt before. I kept praising the Lord, and suddenly I wasn't speaking English anymore! I was praising God effortlessly in a heavenly, unknown tongue. The Lord Jesus was baptizing me in His Holy Spirit. It was wonderful!

Remember now, I was only seven, and knew little about this Pentecostal experience. But no one had to tell me that what was happening to me was from God. (In the midst of this heavenly experience, I didn't feel hungry anymore!)

So there in the front seat of the car, traveling along a country road in Pennsylvania, I was filled with the Holy Spirit and spoke in tongues.

My Dad was working the evening shift that night, so on our way home, we stopped to pick him up. By now, it was midnight and I was still speaking in my heavenly language. This wonderful experience continued until 4 a.m. Friend, this was the greatest experience of my life.

Now, over forty years later, this same Holy Spirit is still operating in my life with power and authority. I can surely testify to the truth of Psalm 107:9, which reads, *He satisfies the longing soul, and fills the hungry soul with goodness.*

I hope you are hungry for this Pentecostal experience. I hope you are excited about what you can have through the indwelling Holy Spirit. This Pentecostal experience is for all believers. It is for **you**. Just believe, receive, **and** be filled now! God bless you!

Bibliography

The Preacher's Homiletic Commentary. Grand Rapids: Baker Book House, 1980.

The Holy Bible. The New King James Version. Thomas Nelson Publishers: Nashville, 1982.

The Living Bible. Wheaton: Tyndale House, 1984.

Hayford, Jack W., Ed. *The Spirit-Filled Life Bible.* Nashville: Thomas Nelson, 1991.

Thompson, Frank C. *Original King James Version.* Indianapolis: B. B. Kirkbridge, 1964.

Hindson, Edward E. and Woodrow M. Kroll. *Parallel Bible Commentary.* Nashville: Thomas Nelson, 1994.

About the Author

Gary Barnhart (b. 1946), a native of Alverton, Pennsylvania, graduated from Hempfield Area High School in 1964. He continued his education with the Assemblies of God, Craig Bible Institute, and the Church of God (Cleveland, TN). Prior to entering full-time ministry, Pastor Barnhart successfully managed retail grocery and restaurant businesses. For five years, he owned a Giant Sub Restaurant in Bangor, Maine.

Pastor Barnhart is ordained as an Evangelist-Pastor with the Church of God. He has evangelized across America with his denomination and has pastored a number of Church of God congregations. He has served on the Chicago Metro Evangelism Board and has been a district Youth Director. He served as a District Overseer for the Church of God in California and pastored in Southern California. He currently pastors in Reno, Nevada. Over the years, he has conducted seminars on the family and has preached the message of salvation and God's miracle working power through radio and television.

Pastor Barnhart and Helen, his wife of over thirty years, have two children and two grandsons.